MENDED

From Broken to Beautiful

A STORY OF REDEMPTION

RL HARNISH

UNITED HOUSE

ISBN: 978-1-952840-18-0

UNITED HOUSE Publishing
Waterford, Michigan
info@unitedhousepublishing.com
www.unitedhousepublishing.com

Book design:
Matt Russell, Marketing Image, mrussell@marketing-image.com

Printed in the United States of America
2022—First Edition

SPECIAL SALES
Most UNITED HOUSE books are available at special quantity discounts when purchased in bulk by corporations, organizations, and special-interest groups. For

*To my mom: Your life, your love, your struggles,
and your hope has forever changed my life.*

CONTENTS

INTRODUCTION

I don't know you. I don't know your story, and I surely don't know what led you to buy this book and start reading it. But, given the fact you are reading this, I assume you want to fix your life in some way—you want something more. Despite what society may tell you, there is never a *good* time to start creating something more or a good time to start healing from something that feels broken. Every day is both a hard day to start and the perfect day to start. The work you put into creating a better life will sometimes feel brutal. But even though the work will be excruciating at times, if you are reading this, today is the perfect day to start. You just have to ask yourself the question: What led you here?

Do you feel broken and are desperately searching for ways to put your life back together? Maybe your marriage is on the rocks (or it has ended), your best friend has died, your parents abused you, a friend betrayed you, your child ran away, your pet died...or maybe it's you. Maybe you are breaking your own heart with the constant aftermath of poor decision-making, and you are searching for some way to put yourself back together again.

Maybe it is none of that.

You don't have to feel broken to keep asking yourself if there is something more to life. This is for each of you, every single person who wants something more. The broken, bored, or the one already on the path to fulfillment. I don't know why you are here, but we are here together. I didn't sit down to write this book because I have a doctorate degree in Psychology. I am sitting here because I have been there. I have had a beautiful life, full of hope and ambition. I have had a dull life in which I constantly questioned what on earth I am here to accomplish. I have been broken and shattered, feeling like I could never be put back together. I have felt all these things all at once. One thing about me, though, is I am always searching for something more out of it all.

For decades, I have been picking up broken pieces and somehow mending those pieces together to create something with purpose. I have done it a thousand times, and I will probably be doing it a thousand more times. In mundane times, I am searching for a lesson in the stillness. In the broken times, I am trying to find the lesson in the pain. When everything feels perfect, I want to pause and appreciate it and take notes on how to make it last. That is why I am here. I have been learning lessons and taking notes for years. How can we make something more out of our crazy and beautiful life? We learn to appreciate our good moments, embrace our hardest times, learn how to build on our foundation, own up to mistakes, forgive, be intentional, and break the cycle. Every chapter is written because I have always asked myself, "What can I get out of this?" Every lesson and answer I have received is outlined here for you.

So where to start? Let's start by saying we are all at rock bottom. The encouraging part about being at this place in the journey is that our lives can only go up from this point. Rock bottom is the place where miracles are made.

I read an article by author Glennon Doyle[1] where

she discussed rock bottom, but more specifically, the valleys. There are mountaintops and valleys. No one wants to be in the valley, right? The main goal is always to get to the top of the mountain. When we look at this imagery with the mountain as your metaphor for life, the top of the mountain is where the most successful and happiest people are. The top is where your purpose is fulfilled, where you have a great thriving family, landed a big job, or where you are the healthiest version of yourself—whatever your dream is.

We want to get to the mountain top, and we want to get there fast. But most of us seem to start in these dang valleys. It is unavoidable and necessary to walk through the valley to start your trek up the mountain. In her article, Glennon reminds us even though our goal is the mountaintop, the valleys have beautiful sights. You see the dream here. The valley is your powerhouse, where you gain strength and gather your tools to start climbing that mountain. We don't have to rush out of the place we are in. Let's spend some time in the valley, or at rock bottom. We can admire the view of the mountaintop, but we will not start our climb to the top until we are ready. Let's build up our wisdom and strength first. We are right where we need to be.

Each chapter in this book is broken down into two sections. The first section is my story in narrative form. I tell you everything—the heartbreak, the abandonment, the thrilling times, and the awakenings. The second section of the chapter is the wisdom I gained from that specific season of life and how to apply that wisdom to your own life. In my thirty-one years, I have gone through a lot. At least what I consider to be a lot. For so long, I struggled with why hardships were happening to me. As I got older, I struggled with mistakes I had made and the deep shame that came along with those mistakes. I wanted the picture-perfect life I saw other people experiencing. I didn't think it was fair I had to carry such heartache, resentment, or loneliness when there were other people living such blithe, easy-going lives. Eventually, though, my mindset started shifting.

As I got older, I had the foresight to understand that the trials I had endured would better equip me to handle future obstacles. I looked around and realized that at some point everyone I knew had experienced heartache on some level. Then, it occurred to me, as a result of going through those struggles and applying the lessons from them, I could more easily handle the trials that life threw at me. Don't get me wrong-the afflictions we all face often are not fair, deserved, or enjoyable. But, when we can look at these struggles in a new way, as something that makes us stronger instead of something that wounds us, we can use that strength to see a future filled with hope instead of hurt.

My hope is, when you read this book, you can tell just how much I appreciate every little, big, beautiful, and painful moment. There are times in my life I don't want to relive, but I am thankful for them and the lessons learned. Because of these moments, I have become a better person who wants *you* to be a better person. The stories I tell and the memories I share are my own. I have asked a few people in my life to clarify some details, but they are mostly from me. Any mistake is unintentional, but my perception has shaped my memory and reality. All names have been changed to protect others' privacy. Nothing in this book is meant to cause heartache or shame to anyone, including me. We all battle demons. We all have the thing we wish we could take back. But we can't take anything back. What we can do is grow from the experience. The Bible says, "Consider it pure joy...whenever you face trials of many kinds because you know that the testing of your faith produces perseverance. Let perseverance finish its work so that you may be mature and complete, not lacking anything" (James 1:2-4, NIV). My friends, let's take these trials and count them as joy TODAY. Let's rejoice at the fact that you have battled demons, gone through heartache and rejection. We will go through your battles together, and through your perseverance of facing them and learning from them, you will gain so much more in the end. You will have the wisdom and strength to continue on, no matter what life throws at you.

We are only at the beginning, so we all will have a lot of work to put in. We will recall some of our best times and prepare for some of our worst. Each chapter will provide a takeaway you can immediately use as a power tool to get you up the mountain you are wanting to climb. There will be easy chapters and hard chapters. But if you get through the work in each chapter, you will come out stronger. It's time to get something more out of this crazy, beautiful life and mend these broken pieces. Let's get started.

One

FIND THE GOOD

I like to ask people, "What's your very first memory?" I am not trying to find some deeper meaning in it; I am genuinely curious. Mine took place in a Walmart dressing room. I had to be about two at the time, and it was during one of our weekly shopping trips. I was excited. I remember feeling like my mom would be *so* proud of me for learning why people went into the dressing rooms. I had finally figured it out: dressing rooms are for people to get naked, and I was going to show her how clever I was. I took off every piece of clothing I had on, stood proudly in the mirror, and took off running. I have no idea how far I got or how many people saw my naked, shrieking self, but I can only imagine how mortified my mom must have been. You know the saying, "What goes around comes around"? I have four children now who all think it is hilarious to strip down and run outside to play. Payback is something else.

I have a few memories from when I was a toddler. I know I was two or three because they all took place in the first home we lived in. Most are brief flashes of a memory, like waiting for my brother at his bus stop or running down the porch steps to the ice cream truck. When I think of those times, I instantly smile. As a parent now, I have an even greater appreciation for those two-second memories. They aren't spectacular memories. We weren't on a fancy vacation or holiday. Out of hundreds of thousands of memories my little mind could have held onto, the two memories that stuck with me for twenty-plus years are the most mundane, simple, yet peaceful memories one can have. What a beautiful reminder as a parent that we don't have to fill our children's lives with lavish things or special occasions. Instead, we can fill up their day-to-day life with simple gestures of love. As a small child and now an adult, nothing beats those brief memories of a hug from my brother and an ice cream treat from my mom.

As I grew up and my memory bank started expanding, I held onto details. I noticed my mom and dad frequently fighting. I did not like staying with babysitters, including my brother. I did not want anyone but my mom (or occasionally my grandma and aunt) to watch me. I hated seeing my mom leave for work or an errand, but I especially hated seeing her leave to shut the bedroom door to fight with my dad. It is incredible for so much time to have passed, yet I still remember how I felt and what I heard during those nights. What parents don't realize is that sometimes their absence allows for a different kind of heartache to trickle in-whether they shut the door to fight, when they walk away to use drugs, when they disappear into their own depression or anger, or when they sink into work as an escape. Sometimes parents may think they are protecting their children from seeing their pain. But from their absence, a new pain forms; a pain that is only subdued by protection and love.

I'm going to go off on a tangent. There is a meaning behind this completely unrelated story; I promise. We have chickens. Well, we had chickens. The final one died last week. We have a large, fenced-in backyard that backs up to a protected forested area. We live in a neighborhood with an HOA, but our house is in the prime location to have chickens because of how secluded our backyard is. We had a coop for them to sleep in at night, but during the day they roamed the yard and chased the kids while they played. Every single night, right as the sun went down, we would walk outside to put them into their coop. We are amateur chicken owners, so in the few blogs we read on raising chickens, it always said to put them in their coop at night. We weren't really sure why though. They couldn't jump our fence, our yard is secluded, and most of the time they went to the coop by themselves.

Night after night, we would walk out and put them into their coop. All except one night. It was a baseball game night; we all had arrived back home exhausted, and it was way past bedtime. We didn't even think about the chickens before we fell into our beds and passed out. The next morning, when we woke up and realized we hadn't put the chickens to bed, we panicked and ran outside. But there they were, all our chickens happily running around the yard. We didn't plan to let our guard down because we knew we were supposed to protect them, but it was okay because they were all there. Then, a week later, the same series of events happened. We woke up and panicked, but alas, they were still safe. After the second time, we let our guard down and everything was fine, we realized it wouldn't be a big deal if we forgot sometimes. Clearly, the chickens didn't need our protection. We knew what we read, but we left them twice without anything happening, so it wasn't a major deal to not lock them in their coop at night.

About two weeks later, when we felt comfortable about not locking them up at night, we woke up to what looked like a feathered bomb had gone off outside. There were feathers everywhere. They were on the deck, on the fence, on the swing set, the ground...and there was one less chicken. From that point on, the chickens were taken out, one by one, by some unknown predator, lurking in the woods, waiting for any opportunity to snatch one up.

It seems dramatic, but that's how I felt when my mom left me. I'm not talking about her abandoning me but simply leaving me for a few hours with a babysitter. I wanted to be around my mom the way most little girls desire. I was little, and she was my everything in life. Most of the time, she only left to go to work. Rarely, she would leave me so she could run an errand. I would beg her not to go. I would cry, scream, and kick, but eventually, she would leave. And when she came back from that first time gone, she came back to everything perfectly fine. I was safe. It happened again and again until she was comfortable with my babysitter. But as soon as she let her guard down, as we did with the chickens, something unexpected happened.

My mom had left to go to the store this time, and as usual, I did not want her to go. I hated staying with the babysitter, and I wanted her to see my desperation to be with her. But I guess all kids get like that at some point: clingy to their mom. The fighting between her and my dad was happening often now, and I had to stay alone with the babysitter too much for my liking. This time, when she left, I decided to take matters into my own hands. As soon as the babysitter looked away, I bolted out of the door and ran as fast as I could down the road to get to my mom. I had no idea where she was, but I knew I was going to get to her. I got a few houses away, still running as fast as I could when BAM! Something hit me, and I was instantly knocked to the ground. I could not get up, because when I tried, I realized I was stuck. A CAR WAS DIRECTLY OVER MY BODY. I pushed my little face far into the ground and stayed there. With a mouth full of dirt and what felt like an eternity had passed, I finally opened my eyes again. I was being held by neighbors, and before I knew it, my mom was rushing back to scoop me up in her arms.

I thought, from that point on, she would never leave me again. But as the fighting between her and my dad got worse, she had to leave me more. I started blaming my dad for it. Every time she left me alone, I felt I was in danger. The car incident proved my point. Without her with me, everything seemed dangerous-a creepy babysitter, busted knee, wasp sting, a grumpy old neighbor. Silly things I can't help but laugh at as an adult. But as a child, I felt like my life was in chaos and full of risks if my mom wasn't hovering to protect me. I know she was trying to shelter me from seeing her own pain, but I hated every second I was without her. Because of that, when she and my dad finally split up, I barely even noticed. In fact, I felt relieved. I truly loved my dad; my mom even said I was a daddy's girl. But nothing compared to how much I needed my mom. If my dad leaving meant I didn't have to be alone with a babysitter, or have to hear them fight, I gladly took that part of the deal.

Besides a few memories, I don't have any other memory of my dad until later in life. He and my step-brother quietly slipped away from my life and my memories. I honestly appreciated it because I never had anyone to miss. I am sure there was an adjustment period for my mom and me, but it doesn't stand out. I thought a two-person family was normal. One child and one parent, and I was content. The closed doors and screaming were now a thing of the past. I was a happy little girl. Dramatic and strong-willed, but happy.

My mom was a bartender for most of my childhood. While I grew to hate it because of the late nights, she did great for herself as a single mother. I never went without anything. She was able to attend field trips and eat lunch with me often;

MENDED

I felt like I had something the other kids didn't. I would come home from school, and we would watch a soap opera, *As the World Turns*, while she got ready. Even after all these years, I cherish those memories with her. It was nothing special, just our daily routine, but I looked forward to the hour after school watching TV with her. I even enjoyed sitting at the bar waiting for my grandma to come to get me. The bar was empty, and as my mom prepped for her shift, I would fill up the ice container for her, and she would give me a cherry coke as a treat. Those simple memories warm so much of my heart. Once my grandma picked me up, I would stay with her until my mom was done with work in the wee hours of the morning. My mom would take me home to my bed, only to have to wake up an hour or two later to get me ready for school. In all honesty, I don't think I ever fully appreciated the effort it took for her to do all that every single night. How much easier would it have been to let me spend the night? My grandma insisted I could stay over, but my mom was determined for me to remember only being raised by her. She was determined to make it as a single mom. And guess what? I remember it.

Because my dad wasn't part of my life, neither was his family. When I say my family, I only ever mean my mom's side. My mom grew up with two brothers and a sister. My grandfather was a Merchant Marine, so he lived on a ship during much of their childhood. He was retired and always around by the time I was born, so I didn't understand our unconventional family dynamic as a child. My grandparents came from deep, southern Christian roots, where customarily, the man is the head of the household. However, our family didn't follow those rules. I guess because my grandfather was away so much of their childhood, my mom and her siblings knew my grand*mother* was the leader of our pack. She was

18

the rule-maker, advice-giver, and the biggest cheerleader for all of us. If she said we would all eat lunch together every single Sunday, you'd better believe that is exactly what we did. There were all kinds of dysfunction in their household. But somehow, we were all always together. Grandma's rules.

I don't remember many people outside of my family as a child. My cousins were my best friends. My older cousin was my idol; I wanted to be like her. She was beautiful, hip, had the best handwriting, and the coolest friends. She is eight years older than me, so she got to boss me around, and of course, I obliged. I had to scratch her back every night for what felt like hours, and somehow, my back scratch only lasted a second. As a teenager, she would let me feel like the coolest kid ever by letting me hang out with her and her friends. I think she liked having me with her too—babysitting me was always a good excuse to have some freedom, and I was the best secret keeper.

I am slightly older than my other cousin. He was like my little brother, and he was my best friend. Even though our family was a tight-knit group, there were times when it felt like he and I were all we had. Rocky relationships and addictions run deep in our blood, and it seemed one of those was always happening. We didn't understand it all then, but I believe children understand even more than adults on some levels. We didn't know the details, but we could feel the tension, anger, and loneliness. Some days, we thought we could be happier if it were only me and him. We thought about our life without adults all the time, and one day, being typical kids, we decided we would run away.

I guess we weren't exactly typical though because we decided we would need to become dogs to run away. Dogs were happy. Dogs were loved by everyone, and they also got to play whenever they wanted. We shoveled handfuls of dog food into our mouths and sat and prayed that would be enough to change us forever. We were utterly disappointed when it was time to go inside and we had to walk on our own two human legs to do it.

Sometime in early elementary school, my mom started dating again. Once she entered the dating world, there were multiple men in and out of my life for many years. Each stayed long enough for us to develop some type of relationship. It was strange to me at first. It had only ever been the two of us, and now someone else was a part of that. The first man I remember made our life a living hell. His name was John. Once he came into the picture, life changed. My mom and I moved out of our house and into John's. His daughter also lived there on his designated weekends. There isn't much I remember about him aside from the yelling I could hear outside of my bedroom door.

I have no idea how long they were together, but it was entirely too long. When they fought, it wasn't small arguments. It was physically, verbally, and emotionally damaging. He often locked my mom out of the house for no reason. I would be left inside, and he would taunt us by telling her we would be separated permanently. We would scream for each other through the thin trailer walls. Some of those nights, he would give in and push me out with her, leaving us both outside in the pitch black, freezing cold of the night. During another fight, when he was feeling particularly malicious, he had me sit inside with him as he tossed all our family pictures into the fireplace. As I watched the images of our smiling faces transform into ash, I listened to the pounding of my mom's fist against the aluminum walls, begging to come back inside. Up until very recently, when I embraced the concept of forgiveness, he claimed the title in my head as the only person I had ever hated.

Scott was the second man I met, and he was wealthy, which was great at first. We took vacations to the mountains and spent summers at his pool. But most importantly, my mom seemed happy. No one in my family had traveled much, so it was heartening to see him take my mom to Las Vegas and Mexico. Even though her life seemed better, looking back, I can tell I wasn't aware of everything happening around me. We quickly moved into Scott's house, just like John's.

Although he had a big house, and his kids only visited on holidays, I never had a bedroom. I slept on the couch for some time, until they got a daybed for me. He didn't speak to me much, and I always felt like I didn't belong. I didn't like it there. I was bored and lonely. I couldn't play with anything that belonged to his kids, and I didn't have anyone to play with. Because I was young, I was shielded from the details, but for some reason, my family did not like us at his house either. Even though John was abusive, something about Scott made my family very concerned.

The transition happened overnight. One day I was living my life surrounded by my aunts, uncles, cousins, and grandparents, and the next day, it was just me, my mom, and Scott. Us and the constant flow of child protective service agents, police officers, and teachers keeping me after class to ask questions about my life at home and my mom's relationship. I couldn't comprehend any of it. All I was told was my family (my grandparents and aunt) wanted to take me away from my mom. Honestly, I still can't identify the exact factors that caused it. I do not remember anything significant that would trigger it, aside from my living room bedroom. My mom and I would hold each other at night, crying and praying it wouldn't be the last night that we would have each other. When my teachers questioned me after class, I knew what to say. I would tell them all how mean and scary all of my family was. Even though I was young, I knew how crucial it was to protect my mom, despite it meaning I had to sacrifice my yearning to see my family. I desperately missed them, but I loved my mom more.

The sudden custody battle terrified me. The day of the trial felt like doomsday. I knew, on that day, I would go to school like any other day. But it wouldn't be any other day because when I left school, someone would be waiting for me ready to determine my fate. If my mom were there, that would mean she had won the case. If it were anyone else, I wouldn't know when or if I would see my mom again. I walked out of school that day trembling with fear, but when I looked up, my mom was right there waiting for me. She'd won the case, and there was no one who could separate us again. I also knew that because of the trial, I would undoubtedly never see my family again, but as long as I had my mom, it didn't matter.

Unexpectedly, exactly one week after the court case, my grandfather died of a massive heart attack. As soon as we got the news, my mom mercifully forgave all my family and reunited with them for his funeral. I vividly remember the tense, awkward feeling of reconnecting with my aunt, uncles, cousins, and grandma. We didn't talk about what had happened. We moved on like the hell we had gone through for months never happened. It wasn't long before we all found our new normal and we were back at Grandma's for Sunday lunches.

The custody trial was devastating for my family, but some good came out of it. It eventually led to my mom and Scott ending their relationship, and my mom and I were able to start fresh again. We moved into a pretty apartment in a small town and started over—for the third time. This time, though, our new home brought healing. Home became a refuge instead of a prison.

The dating cycle picked right back up, though, and my mom met someone new. The first time I met her new boyfriend, I hated him. He had long hair, drove a motorcycle, and he didn't even make my mom wear a helmet. As a kid, I thought it was reckless and irresponsible. I wanted no part of knowing this man, but when she came back safe and smiling, I figured maybe this guy wasn't the worst person ever. I would give him a little chance. Brandon was my favorite chance I had ever taken. He was not just her boyfriend. For the first time, my mom was not the only person he cared about in the family. He cared about me, too.

He was the missing piece I hadn't realized was ever missing. I liked him so much because he was more than a person in our house—he was an active part of my life. We played games together, he helped me with homework, made me a Halloween costume, and came to my school events. He even came to those special Father's Day breakfasts that the school held. My school called it Doughnuts For Dad. Doughnuts For Dad had always been one of those events that made me feel lonely, but not anymore. I finally had my person, and I was eager to show him off. I loved every minute of him being in our life. I ate up the attention.

Brandon wasn't only my mom's boyfriend; he was the one who came and changed our lives completely. He showed us love and happiness. Even as a kid, I expected the newness to wear off at some point. But even when the honeymoon phase was over, he stayed. When they did have arguments, they weren't screaming matches and abuse. The arguments ended...and he still stayed. He stayed so long, relationship drama became a thing of the past. We were a family.

Our hearts were healed and whole.

Why Does This Even Matter?

Rebuilding your life, more specifically your heart takes some soul searching. When I think about rebuilding something, I often think of renovating a house. I have never renovated one, so I might have all the steps wrong, but bear with me. If we were to buy an old run-down house to renovate and rebuild, what would your first step be? For me, it would be to find the beauty of the house as it is right at that moment before any construction starts. As far as a home renovation goes, the buyer must first find something they like about the house before they pick apart all the things that are wrong and broken. I would look around and identify the beautiful parts of the house we'd want to keep before going in and doing a full demolition. I want to use the same approach when we begin rebuilding our hearts and lives.

I told you the story of my life starting from my first memory to early childhood for a reason. When I look at the whole picture of my early childhood now as an adult, all I can see is how chaotic and unstable those years were: bouncing houses, fights, different men, and witnessing abuse. But if I think back on my childhood and remember it the way I felt as I was living it then, childlike and innocent, I still see the good parts. Childhood is so special and precious because children look for happiness everywhere they go, even the children who go through horrific times. Do you know what is equally special and precious? *We were those children*. No matter what your childhood looked like, whether there was death, rape, drugs, neglect…you, as a child, found enough beauty to keep going.

I know that because you are here now, reading this. Think of your life as an old, broken house we are going to work hard to rebuild and find beauty in.

Let's start by asking some questions about your childhood. What made you happy? What do you remember about those happy times? It seems silly at first; sometimes it could even feel daunting. How could you possibly remember those simpler, happier times when all you see is the _____ (Insert your own traumatic event or bad memory)? I want you to think like you are a child, still innocent and looking for little pieces of happiness to get you through. Maybe you remember your parents screaming at each other. What were you doing during those times? Did you go play with a neighbor? Call your best friend? Color? Hide in your room and play with your dolls? Those coping tools may not seem effective now, but it gives insight to *how* you initially cope. That is how and where I want you to start healing your brokenness.

As adults, we have the insight to understand what was happening around us as children. But as children, we were innocent enough to search for happiness, even in the darkest of times because we didn't fully understand how dark those times really were. The Bible tells us to return to that childlike state: "unless you change and become like little children, you will never enter the kingdom of heaven." (Matthew 18:2, NIV). The Bible unquestionably views children as the purest form of human life. To become like little children, we have to view the world, our life, and our past through the lens of a child.

As children, we find happiness within the smallest things. As children, we love without question. As children, we have endless faith and hope for a better tomorrow. If you can peel back the layers of hurt, pain, and anger, and see the happiness you held onto as a child, you can start rebuilding your life by using that happiness. This part is as crucial to rebuilding your life as it is to renovate a house. We will have to tear down and destroy so many pieces, but we will always be able to have a piece to look at for beauty on our journey.

To get something greater out of your life, you have to do the work. Hard work. However, I want to share with you a quote I heard years ago and has stuck with me ever since: "Hard is *not* the same as bad." Digging into your past might hurt, but it will bring forth growth. This is *good*, beautiful, worthwhile work to put into your life and your future. When you are doing this, I want you to look at the examples because sometimes it is impossible to fully recreate the memories that remind you of good times, and sometimes you may not want to recreate them at all. When you think back on your happiest memory, and it is with someone who is no longer around, you will have to figure out the next best thing. If playing with Barbies was your escape as a 6-year-old, I can imagine it probably won't bring the same amount of happiness as an adult. We are not attempting to recreate exact memories. It is about recreating the feeling of happiness and figuring out *why* it sparks joy for you.

Here is your life application for this chapter:

Step 1: Think back to your childhood and write down three specific memories that brought happiness (examples: calling a friend, playing outside, coloring, visiting family).

Step 2: Unpack these memories. We need to figure out what it was about these memories that brought joy. This step can feel weird to people, which is okay. It might feel strange to unpack coloring in your room, but honestly, there *is* something to unpack in an event as simple as that. Did you like being alone and de-stressing by coloring and writing? What about other happy times? Did specific traditions bring happiness, such as getting pizza on Fridays? Maybe going to a friend's house for a sleepover? Once you pick a few things that brought you true happiness, think about why they made you happy. If your comforting memories are based on specific events, like holidays at grandma's or pizza on Fridays, it might be traditions or routines that brought you the stability you craved. If your memories involve being alone or having friends over, the comfort you felt might have a lot to do with whether you are an introvert or extrovert. You might need to either be alone or be around people to recharge for a little bit. No matter what the memory is, there *is* something deeper in the memory that brought happiness and peace to your life as a child.

I feel like I could write an entire chapter based on this single bullet point. This step means you must really figure out who you are as a person. If you are having trouble unpacking these memories and figuring out *why* they brought you joy, then I want to suggest some tools to help you get to know yourself a little better. First, comes figuring out if you are an introvert or extrovert, knowing if you recharge through being alone or being around people. Next, I would figure out your enneagram number (www.enneagramtest.net). Enneagram is basically a personality test, but it really dives into your core desires and what specific things bring you happiness and fulfillment. Last, I would take the love language quiz and figure out your love language (5lovelanguages.com). Some of your best memories might be based on someone showing you love exactly the way you crave it. Unless you have taken the quiz, you may not understand, nor have you been able to convey to others the way you need love to be expressed to you. I encourage you to go to these websites and take the five-minute quizzes. I do strongly feel like the more you know about yourself, the easier it becomes to know the specific things that bring fulfillment to your life and why you cherish those memories so much.

Step 3: List ways to recreate these memories. This step is virtually impossible unless you have done step two. You can't recreate an exact memory. No matter how hard we wish, we can't bring grandma back from heaven and recreate the year 1990 on Christmas morning with the family. But if you have unpacked it, you might realize that even though, yes, you loved Grandma and your cousins and believing in Santa, it was: A. family time, B. the tradition of going to a specific place on a specific holiday, or C. getting a gift, that made you feel loved. If you can narrow down the root of the feeling to one or more of those, then, you can essentially recreate, not that exact moment, but another similar feeling of happiness for yourself. Knowing your love language, Enneagram number, and if you are an introvert or extrovert, can help you figure out why it was a favorite memory and how to mimic it.

Step 4: Go do it!

My personal example:

1. Pick a memory:
Playing with my cousin outside, pretending to be dogs, and getting dirty in the mud.

2. Unpack why it brought joy:
Quality Time is my love language. I am also an introvert, but I thrive on strong connections with specific people. Doing a

specific activity with someone I deeply care about recharges me. On the other hand, being around lots of people or someone I don't deeply connect with and making small talk, drains me.

3. Ways to recreate it:
I can't recreate these exact memories with my cousin because they wouldn't bring the same happiness. We aren't as close as we were as children. So, while I can't recreate that silly moment with my cousin, I can recreate how it made me feel. Since I know my love language is quality time, and I realize this specific memory brings me happiness, I can recreate quality time with a close friend or family member. Examples would be taking a hike with my husband, a dinner conversation with a close friend, or making a craft with my daughter.

Example from a friend:

1. Pick a memory:
Going on weekend trips to see cousins.

2. Unpack why it brought joy:
He is an enneagram 5 (The Observer). This means he is insightful and curious. 5s enjoy research and learning new skills. He is also an Introvert that needs time alone to recharge, but quality time with loved ones is his love language.

From this, he is able to understand that he enjoyed exploring and learning about new places while spending intentional quality time with the people closest to him.

3. How one can recreate it:
Research a new place, and ask someone they care about to go

on a small day trip to a new town, place, or attraction.

Example from a friend:

1. Pick a memory:
Holidays with the family.

2. Unpack:
She is an enneagram 8 (The Challenger). Enneagram 8s are assertive, confident, and strong-willed. She is an extrovert that feels happiest around others. Her love language is getting gifts and quality time. Things that made the memory joyful were the planned time with family, being around people, and getting gifts.

3. How they can recreate it:
An enneagram 8 is decisive and likes to control their environment. To them, planning out specific traditions for the family would allow them to purposefully create these memories and get quality time with family. Examples include Taco Tuesday, strawberry picking in the summer, creating specific events that make holidays special and lead up to the actual day (advent calendars). Since this person's love language is receiving gifts, she is able to use this as a tool in her relationships. Her husband often gives her small gifts to express his love for her.

Those are three examples of recreating the happiness you had as a child. Give it a shot, and try to infiltrate some happiness into your life, even if you think your life is messy and different than it once was. No, it won't be the exact memory, but recreating something familiar has deep roots in your happiness. It is our little piece of beauty in an old, broken home. It is special, sentimental, and full of blissful feelings.

I have to tell you something real though. Recreating these deep-rooted feelings of happiness is great; I truly believe sometimes you need to remember how to find those simple joys again. But, if you are a believer, there is joy and peace found in knowing God. There are scriptures such as Psalm 16:11, NIV "You make known to me the path of life; you will fill me with joy in your presence…" and Jeremiah 15:16, NIV, "When your words came, I ate them; they were my joy and my heart's delight" that give us hope that we may have joy in just *knowing* God and being in His presence through prayer or reading His word. That promise is everlasting. Keep that in your mind as you work through this chapter, as we talk about happiness, and the next chapter, when we talk about pain. Knowing how to find joy at all times in life, even in times of suffering, is a game-changer when it comes to creating a better life. Do the work in this chapter to find a simple joy, even in the darkest of times, and turn that joy into hope for a better tomorrow.

Two

ACCEPT YOUR PAIN

Brandon was our everything. With him came stability I had never experienced before, and I didn't take it for granted. I soaked up the attention. He was a hands-on type of person, and this reflected in everything he did in life. When I had a project, he was the one beside me coming up with the best ideas. I even won first place in third grade during Black History Month for recreating the scene of Rosa Parks on the bus with the back of an old Barbie box. My mom and I would look at each other in amazement after we were done because we knew we would have never had the vision to even begin. That was who he was though. He was always submerging himself in a project of some kind. We developed a bond through his projects, and I loved being his helper.

Middle school opened my eyes to the world around me. Maybe that's when things began to get rocky for them, or maybe it was when I started noticing. My mom and Brandon had a large group of friends they often went out with. At first, it was family cookouts with their friends, but over time, it became late-night drinking at the bar. It wasn't long until those late nights also meant there would be a morning argument to accompany. The arguments increased over time, and before long, it felt like the tension in the house was palpable. The arguments in the other room were awkward for me to listen to with teenage ears. My innocent mind was gone, and I knew what they were arguing about. For the longest time, I believed they were immune to arguments and breaking up. My mom had already had her fair share of bad relationships, so I thought there was no way they could split up. In my eyes, they were a match made in heaven. When I heard the arguments shift from nitpicking to infidelity, my heart sank. I knew then it was a real possibility that our dream life could come to an end.

As the arguing increased, I held out hope that a vacation we had planned would put an end to any problems they may have had. Our vacation came and it was wonderful and argument-free. It almost felt magical because, in my heart, I knew things were ending, but everything seemed perfect while we were there. But as the vacation ended, and summer wrapped up, reality sank in for the final time. Vacation didn't heal their relationship; it was over. There weren't any screaming matches like my Mom's previous relationships; just tears. There was nothing that could help the situation this time.

He wasn't going to fight back. Brandon was done and nothing could be said to salvage the six years they'd spent together. He had been taking his things piece by piece for days, but there was a final night when he was to come to get the remaining items left at the house. After this night, our house would be like he was never there at all. I braced myself for a bad night. My mom was crumbling minute by minute, and even as a teenager, I knew this was going to make her fall apart. I just didn't know how.

At first, it was calm, she told him she loved him and needed him. I heard her remind him of the good times they had spent together and how often they'd laughed with one another. But while she talked, he kept packing his bags. She started crying, then begging, which turned into sobbing. She was drenched in tears and pulling at his clothes. Her desperation was intense, almost as if she were fighting for him to take another breath.

I was just an observer on the other side of the room. At first, I was there to say my own goodbye, hoping he would tell me this wasn't the end of the two of us. But, I don't even think they knew I was there. She only saw him, and he only saw a way out. I was detached, seemingly unphased, but inside, my world was falling apart. This was my fault. I didn't enjoy vacation, I was a bratty teenager, and I had been grounded for sneaking out of the house with my best friend. Why would he want to stick around to be a father to someone like me? As the night went on, I stayed in my corner and observed the scene before me, burning an indelible memory into my brain.

I remember those last minutes like it was yesterday. My mom was in full panic at this point. He walked out of the bedroom, bags in his hand. He only had the hallway to walk down before he reached the front door, and then it would be over. Forever. There would be no reason to come back after this. She screamed. She cried. She hit him. She was not going to let him get out of the door. She hit him over and over, and I let her do it. I didn't want him to leave either. But then, something in him changed and he wasn't so calm anymore. He was angry she was trying to stop him.

Once I saw the look in his eyes, I knew that this time, he might actually do to her what she was doing to him. I had to step in. I stood between them, so he couldn't hit her back. I held my mom tight, even though she was now trying to fight *me*. I held her long enough for Brandon to get out of the front door and leave. Once he made his way out of the door, she turned to me and told me she hated me. He left as fast as he could, without even a glance back or a goodbye. I was heartbroken but relieved the night was finally over. We both needed to rest.

But we did not rest. The hell had just begun, and the night was young. I sank onto the couch, hoping we could get sleep and wake up to a new beginning. Unfortunately for all of us, my mom wasn't going to rest as we wanted. She was still in full desperation mode. I could hear her in her room, opening every single drawer and fumbling around, and then slamming them closed, frustrated. Open, close, open, close, open, close. I wondered to myself what on earth she was looking for. Then, the slamming stopped, and I didn't hear anything. "Finally," I thought. She was going to bed.

I let her rest for a little bit, hoping I would walk in there in a few minutes to see her sleeping peacefully. When I walked in, though, she was still awake but lying there. At first, I was relieved, but two seconds later, I spotted something that made my heart sink. I saw an empty bottle of pills laying right beside her. I panicked and screamed, "What have you done? What is this?!" She was still coherent but getting groggy at this point. She responded like nothing was wrong. "It is just a bottle of tranquilizers. Everything will be better now." I was young and didn't understand, so I felt relieved. I trusted her when she said everything would be okay. I wanted to believe everything was going to be fine. I watched her closely, unsure of my next move, still trying to process what was happening in front of me. That is when she told me.

"I can't live without him. I took the bottle of pills."

My world started spinning, and I couldn't see straight. My mom was my life, and I was terrified.

She was going to die.

For an instant, I panicked. But in the next moment, I realized I needed to calm down and act fast. I grabbed the phone and dialed 911. I told them exactly what had happened.

I read the label on the bottle and gave them our address. I felt a responsibility to make my mom comfortable. If this was her last moment on earth, I *had* to make it peaceful for her. She was drifting off at this point, so I sat and rubbed her head, telling her I loved her over and over. I didn't tell her to fight or to stay with me. I just wanted to make her happy until the ambulance showed up or until the end. I told her we would see each other in our dreams, and it would all be okay.

The paramedics arrived and took her to the hospital where they pumped her stomach and gave her a psych evaluation. I rode in a police car behind the ambulance to the hospital. My grandma and aunt met me there to take me home. I stayed with my aunt, and a few hours later, when my alarm went off, I was back at school like nothing had happened the night before.

And seven days later, my mom was back at home.

That's how we handled things in our family. If we pretended it never happened, then it didn't.

That night was the beginning of a life we'd never prepared for. But prepared or not, my mom was about to take us on a long, wild ride. Nothing was okay with her when she left the hospital. She was in the worst shape of her life, and without anyone actively checking on her to make sure she was getting better, she quickly spiraled out of control. Her grief turned into substance abuse quickly. I knew something had changed in my mom, but I couldn't grasp the complexity of the situation. I was naïve and didn't think drugs could happen to someone in my life. But the highs and lows were evident. There would be moments during the day that she was cleaning the house, talkative, and happy. Later, she was a completely different woman whom I had never met before. She was mean and irrational. Suddenly, she was getting in fights with everyone, including me. Something was changing her. I just didn't know what.

I was not a little girl anymore, and as I transitioned into high school, my eyes were opened to more outside influence. The more I was aware of the world, the more I realized what was happening within my home was not normal. Thankfully, my mom knew she had a problem and wanted help. She eventually came clean and told my family she was struggling with pain pills. She said when she took the pills, she could finally stop crying and would have the motivation to leave the bed. Over the next five years, after Brandon left, she would go to seven-day detox centers about once a year. I was always so proud of her when she went to these treatments. I knew it had to be difficult to admit a struggle and to ask for help. My mom was openly admitting she had a problem, but besides taking her to that seven-day treatment center, nothing else was done. She would come home, and we would continue life as if they gave her some miracle treatment to cure her of addiction and the pain she was living with.

But that wasn't the case. We could all pretend she'd received a magic cure, but in reality, she was spiraling out of control. Every time she came back from detox, it was like gasoline had been poured on her addiction during her time away. The fire didn't burn when she was gone, but once she was back home and struck the match, it exploded. This time, though, there weren't the highs and lows; she was gone. The high she felt didn't look like my normal, happy, talkative mom to me. The pain pills disguised her. Now, when she was high, she was incoherent.

A flood of new people started coming into our house, and no one cared that I was living at home, still trying to get through school. They partied into all hours of the night and left remnants of their drugs around. My mom was deep in it now. Cable was the first thing gone. Then she started selling random things throughout the house that meant nothing to her. She would go through her clothes and sell those. Sometimes, the water or lights would be off for several days or weeks before my grandma realized and paid the bill for her.

And then, when she was done going through her items, she came for mine. Random clothes would be gone. A lamp would be missing. Then one day, she asked me if I wanted a new bedroom suite. I said yes, of course, even though mine was fine. I was still young and trusted my mom, so I figured she had made a lot of money that week at work; even though, in the back of my mind, I was wondering if she was even still going to work as high as she was getting. The next afternoon, I came home from school to an empty room. There was nothing left in my room besides a mattress on the ground and my clothes scattered on the floor.

Oh.

Right.

I understood now.

There was never a plan for new furniture. There was only the plan to sell the furniture. I got it.

Out of all things, I didn't expect that to be what finally tipped me over my edge, but it did. She took away the only place of comfort I had. During all of this, I had hated being at home. I hated what my mom was doing. I hated the person she was becoming. I never told anyone though because I wanted to protect her. I didn't want her to get in trouble. I spent so many nights locked inside my room, scared of the people on the other side of the door. I spent so much time in bed crying, fearing I would walk out to find my mom dead. But I still felt such a deep loyalty to her that I would tiptoe out of my room after the party ended and check to make sure she was sleeping and breathing. I hated the situation she was in, but I loved her. But now, she took away the only escape I had, my bedroom. The playing field was now different, and I was mad. I knew I had to tell someone what was going on.

It was hard for me to sit and tell on my mom, but shortly after I told my grandma, my mom went to her first long-term treatment center. It was the best and biggest step in the direction of a better life for the two of us; although, I never could have guessed the way things would play out. No one but God would understand the timing of our situation, and the way the next few months played out could only be written by God himself.

One morning, a few months before I had told on my mom, there was a knock on our door. When I opened it, I found my dad and my stepmom, Susan. He told me he had moved back into town and was ready for us to start a new relationship. I honestly didn't even know what to think. I wasn't comfortable around him, and I was skeptical. As I grew older and noticed I didn't have a father like my friends, I began writing a story in my head about why my dad left and what he was doing while he was gone. I knew he was a drinker before he left, so I told myself that he must have traded family life for a life of partying. I never looked for him or sought him out during this time because I thought his life must be even more hectic than my own.

Hesitantly, I agreed to go to lunch with my dad the following day. During lunch, he told me stories about my grandparents that I didn't remember and filled me in on what he had been doing while he was gone. He'd left us because he needed to become a better person. Attempting to change his life for the better in an environment full of partying and instability seemed futile, so he left. He walked away from a life of destruction and into a world of stability and hope. This reality left me shaken. I didn't see what was happening as a young girl. His decision to leave may have not been the best, but at the time, he saw it as his only choice. Even as a teenager, I had the wisdom to understand the desperation of his decision and love him for it. After a few lunch dates, I excitedly welcomed him and my step-mom back into my life.

My dad and his wife were kind and thoughtful. They worked hard to make ends meet and still made time to see me. The timing of their introduction back into my life was divine. My dad had no idea my mom's life was completely spiraling out of control when he showed up at my door. As they began to search for a place to live, my grandma was desperately seeking long-term rehab for my mom. My dad and I became pretty close by this time, so when the question was proposed to my Dad and Susan, asking if they could temporarily move into my house while my mom was away, it seemed too good to be true. I knew it would be a change to the life of freedom I was used to, but at least I wouldn't have to move.

My dad only lived in my house for about six months, but every moment felt like a huge adjustment. My high school life consisted of being with my friends and my boyfriend, and my dad gave me rules as to how often I could do that. Our relationship was always positive, but as a teenager, I couldn't wait until the day my mom moved back in.

When the six months had passed, and the time came for my mom to return home from rehab and my dad and stepmom to move out, our dynamic suddenly shifted. There was tension while life was returning back to normal, and I didn't understand why. The plan had always been temporary. We knew they would move out as soon as my mom was stable enough to move back in. Soon after they moved out, I was asked to go to the courthouse for a mouth swab for "paperwork purposes." I didn't ask a single question and gave the swab as directed. But soon after that, the phone calls from my dad stopped, and any time I tried to call my dad it went straight to voicemail.

One afternoon, my mom called me into her room. I walked in to see her crying. She said she needed to tell me something and that I would be upset. She handed me a paper to read. As soon as I read the header, I knew what it was, but I didn't want to believe what was happening. It felt like the room had disappeared, and my life was flashing before my eyes. I could finally put together pieces of a puzzle I didn't understand as I was growing up. Today, I had been handed the final puzzle piece. In my hand, I had the answers to why the phone calls and lunch dates had stopped. It plainly said my father was not biologically related to me. *He was not my biological dad.* My mom was crying, and my heart was broken. But by that point, I knew how to stay brave for my mom. She never knew how hurt I was over the news because I put on a brave face for her. I told her it was fine and walked out of the room. To this day, we have never spoken of it again.

That day was the day I realized there was actually so much more to life than what I saw while in school. Inside the school building, everyone seemed to be happy and laughing. We talked about hair, weekend plans, and boyfriends. But for me, outside of school was filled with so much pain. At that point, it seemed one thing after the next kept happening in my life that led to heartbreak.

My mom was already back into the same hole she was in before rehab and pretty absent in my life. Suddenly, I felt parentless. I was devastated over the news of my dad because it didn't change how I felt about my dad and Susan. I still loved them. I was devastated because it was evident it changed their feelings towards me. I tried to call them many times after I saw the results on paper, but my calls always went unanswered. Two years passed, and dozens of calls were ignored before we ever talked. Even then, it would take years to ever reestablish any kind of relationship.

The only relationship I felt I truly had was with my boyfriend. We had started dating right before my mom went to rehab, so he was there through most of my trauma. With every hurt I endured, the more I relied on him for my comfort. My friends and family tried to point out the warning signs of how dependent I was on him, but I did not listen to anyone. I started to avoid the advice of my friends at all costs. Any time I was handed a difficult problem or situation, I turned straight to my boyfriend. I didn't see it at the time, but the more I needed from him, the less he wanted me. In all fairness, I needed a lot from him at the time. What I really needed was some type of therapy, but I thought he was the answer to all of my problems. As I felt him pull away from me, I tried to cling tighter. As a result, we started arguing. A lot. He would leave and ignore my calls for hours—sometimes days. This was dreadful for me. I would be stuck crying constantly during those times, praying he would answer and forgive me for whatever I did. Whenever he felt like "forgiving me," things would be back to normal for a while. But, as much as I didn't want to believe it, I knew something was changing.

After months of arguing constantly and crying enough tears to fill a bucket, things with him hit a brick wall. I was supposed to go to his house after school, but when I got there, he wasn't home. I called his phone for hours, but I was sent straight to voicemail. His dad started to panic too, so he started calling his phone for hours with no answer. We were at the point of desperation, about to call hospitals and the police when the door opened, and he walked in. As soon as I saw his face, I knew in my heart what I never would admit to myself. He told us we were overreacting, and he was just driving around. But his face. There was a look of guilt on his face, and when he looked into my eyes, I didn't feel any kind of love from him. I was frantic. I clung to him and tried to get him to tell me where he was, but he would not budge.

The next morning he broke up with me, and two days later, he was dating someone new. After a year and a half with him, solely relying on him for comfort through my chaos, I was now left alone. I was shattered. The pain I was in both physically and mentally was unlike anything I had experienced before—so intense and so deep. I couldn't hold it together. I cried at home, in the car, and at school. The days were agonizing and slow, and making it to bedtime every day seemed like such a huge victory for me. I felt like I had no one in this world and didn't matter to anyone. It was the lowest I had ever been, and at the time, I didn't see a way out.

Why Does This Even Matter?

To say it lightly, trauma presents itself in so many different ways in someone's life. As I sit and write these pages, I am transported back to the night my mom almost took her own life, and I feel those same feelings of panic and despair again. When I think of my own trauma, I also think about the trauma that others have to endure. I think about those people whose parents didn't live to see the same fate as my mom and had died as the result of overdose or suicide. I think about the tragic loss of a family member, or the violence you watched at home, or the rape, or the devastating miscarriage. It seems we all have endured trauma in some way. Whether you think your trauma is more than what others have gone through or a lot less, it still leaves its own unique mark on each of us. The similarity is, no matter who you are, *trauma changes you.*

It is hard to start here in this place because for most people, this place is the entire reason your life was thrown off course. This *is* the reason your heart is shattered. This *is* the reason you started doing drugs. *This* is what caused the divorce—or the divorce was the trauma and caused everything else in life to blow up. Even though it may hurt to revisit this part of your past, we have to look here to initiate the kind of change we want in our lives.

You guys, this is hard work. But it is necessary. To start changing our lives, we must understand why we are in this place of brokenness.

Here is your life application for this chapter:

Step 1: Think of your life, and write out a timeline to piece together events that stand out, both good and bad, mundane and big. You want these to be events that are important to you and shaped your life, whether they were momentous occasions or common, everyday shifts. For my timeline, I need to add little things like high school sports and a family vacation. These events stood out to me because even though they seemed mundane, they were a big part of my heart; without them, my life would have played out differently. For you, a turning point in your life could be a new pet, a failed test, the death of a loved one, not landing your dream job, making the basketball team. Because we will be evaluating when major shifts took place, I would say you need between 5-15 events in your timeline. Too few events, and you won't be able to pinpoint exactly where the shift happened and too many might confuse you.

Here is my example:

Born---dad left, so just mom and me---court case/grandpa died---Mom and Brandon together, trip to Nashville---Brandon leaves, Mom attempted suicide---high school, sports, and friends---boyfriend breaks up with me---graduate/I leave for college---Andy and I start dating---I get into pharmacy school—baby Noah/married/moved home---Adella---grandma sick and dies/Eden/Postpartum/Grief---Remi born, major hemorrhage---ran a half marathon.

To anyone else looking at my list, this might not make any sense. After all, the events that stick out to me and feel important range from high school sports to almost dying during childbirth. My list is broad and complex, but with each event, I changed. Sometimes I changed just a little; like high school soccer taught me persistence and to set goals. Sometimes the event sparked something major. When my dad left, I developed a strong sense of loyalty to my mom that has never faded. Dating Andy was the first time I felt real love.

Every person will have a unique list. Your list doesn't have to be perfect. Your list should be long enough to be able to look at it and walk yourself through your life using only those events. Each event should spark an emotion. Once your list is complete, you can use those events to pinpoint when something prompted a shift in your life. The first step to overcoming anything is to figure out when the shift took place. I am not asking you to dive into the pain and analyze any of it. I don't want us diving into the questions of who or why. I just want us to identify when the turning point in your life happened and what caused it.

Step 2: Take two different colored pens, and use them to highlight or circle each event with those colors. Use one color for happy times and another for painful times. Once you complete this step, take a minute to look over those times. We all go through painful experiences. They are unavoidable. But when you look at your timeline and see the negative experiences clumped together, do you have an ah-ha moment? Do one or two stick out as "the straw that broke the camel's back"? Is that when your lens of life took on a whole new view? When you realized you would never go back to normal?

My happy times were the trip to Nashville, high school, meeting Andy (my now husband), graduating, the births of my children, and accomplishing a major goal (running a half marathon). The bad times were my mom's attempted suicide, my boyfriend breaking up with me, and the death of my grandma. The event that was "the straw that broke the camel's back" and changed me was my grandma's death. Until I made a timeline and started reflecting, I thought I'd handled her death well. And I did handle it well, in the sense of accomplishing tasks and staying strong for others. Making the timeline made me realize my perspective on life immensely shifted after her death. Grief clouded my vision, and my coping mechanisms shifted to negative ones. From that point on, my view of life shifted from hopeful to hopeless.

So many people are good at pushing the bad things to the back of their minds, saying they weren't a big deal. A lot of us, myself included, don't want to admit what caused the pain or what the significance of an event was to us. We tell ourselves other people have it so much worse. *This isn't about them.* This is about you, and this is about coming to terms with what has ultimately changed your life. Only you are living your life, and only you have been shaped by the events that took place and the situations you have been through. This step is best when written out because it is harder to ignore something on paper. If you circled a certain event in your life as painful, ask yourself if it changed you. Did it hurt for a little while before you could move on? Or did it completely change who you were after? Look at your timeline and try to pinpoint when or if there was a shift.

Step 3: Once you identify the major event (or events) that caused a shift in who you are, I want you to draw a branch coming from that specific event. On that branch, write something that has changed within you as a result. Ideally, I would like for you to write how you felt and then an action that resulted from it.

Here's mine:
Mom's attempted suicide: abandonment led to my being overly independent.
Grandma's death: loneliness and devastation led to negative coping mechanisms (alcohol) and disconnection from people.
Remi's birth/major hemorrhage: fragile existence led to feeling empowered to change my life for the better.

The tactics you developed from your painful event are called coping mechanisms. Everyone has them, and they can be good or bad things. Step three can be an eye opener. I always thought I was born emotionally resistant. I thought of myself as cold-hearted. It wasn't until I finally started to do some work on myself and did this step, I realized I was not born this way. I became this way because of the things I had been through and how I responded to them. You do not have to justify your thoughts to anyone or have someone else decide what is small or big to you. Maybe a girl in high school spread a rumor about you, and it ultimately shaped how you now trust people in your adulthood. If that experience changed you, then that is *your truth*. As you navigate through difficulty, you may not see how it is changing you in the moment. Doing "homework" like this, and reflecting on your own personal heartbreaks, can bring light to these experiences. I will say it again so you'll completely understand: you do not have to justify your feelings, experiences, or reactions to *anyone*. If something affected you, it is your truth. The best part and the hardest part about realizing what changed you is that now you get the opportunity to face it and figure out how to use it for good. That is a process that will happen in time though, through unpacking every lesson in this book.

Step 4: Write this sentence: When _____ happened, it made me feel _____. From that experience, I developed this habit/feeling: _____
_____.

Here's mine:
When my mom attempted suicide, it made me feel angry and abandoned. From that experience, I developed a mistrust for people close to me and became very independent.

If this step seems silly to you, I get it. It felt a little silly for me to do it too. But don't underestimate it. We are early into our journey for a mended life, so this step is crucial. Right now, I do not want you to approach the person who hurt you or discover some resolution to this yet. This chapter is simply about uncovering what hurt you in your life and acknowledging how it changed your future. The first step to overcoming anything is to simply acknowledge it. Write this sentence down in your own words, soak it in, and give yourself a pat on the back! You just took a brave look into your past and identified exactly what caused you to feel broken. Knowing where that started is a crucial step to mending the hurt.

Step 5: Find someone (besides the person that caused your hurt or someone directly in contact with that person) to talk to like a therapy session. You knew that was coming, right? I hope, with everything in my soul, you did not pick this book up thinking this would be your therapy session. Listen, I am a woman who has been through a lot and made it out better than I started. But that took so much hard work and way too many years of using bad methods to figure it all out. Once I finally had gotten through my hard times, I was able to write this book to help you along your journey. But it does not go without saying that therapy, whether it is a paid therapist, a teacher, or a friend, is part of it. It is a pillar to overcoming hurt of any kind. It is human nature to talk about your feelings to get relief. Your future self will thank you.

Step 6: Write down those happy events you listed in step 2 on a post-it note. Put it in your wallet or on your mirror so you can periodically read the things you are proud of or bring you joy.

Phew! That was a lot of unpacking of major life-changing events. If you feel like that was too much to take in, please go back and read through each step.

These may appear simple steps, but I know in my heart they are not necessarily easy. These are hurts we have carried with us for months, years, and even decades. We have changed the way we laugh, cry, love our family and our partners, and parent our babies because of these hurts. I am so proud of you for boldly facing the pain in an attempt to overcome these struggles. This work will help you become a whole, mended person. I hope, as you are reading this, you realize you aren't the only person who goes through hardships. This is not saying that your pain isn't big and unique because it absolutely is. But I want you to know you are not alone, and if you search, you will find someone who cares about what you are going through and may have gone through something similar. I hope you continue through this and follow the prompts to someday see the resolution you never thought was possible.

Three

BUILDING UP FROM YOUR FOUNDATION

When I think about my childhood now, I see pure chaos. We moved many times, there were many men, multiple homes, and several arguments with family. Looking back, it was a whirlwind of a life for anyone, especially a child! But even though I look back and see chaos now, I didn't always *feel* it as a child. It wasn't until I was an adult and processed the many events, that I realized my life was chaotic. I believe I didn't feel it as a child because I had such a solid foundation through my religion that disorder wasn't able to shake me too much. In first grade, my life changed so much internally that the outside conditions of my life didn't affect me to the extent they could have.

After my family's big custody battle and the death of my grandfather immediately following, everything became a "new normal." Nothing was quite the same after the tragedy. My grandma rebuilt her life and found a new purpose as a widow. My mom entered the dating world once again. My aunt and uncle's lives changed in a different kind of way, though. They started going to church and were passionate about it. My mom worked Saturday nights, so I normally spent Sunday morning alone playing until she woke up. My aunt and uncle asked if I wanted to join their family at church one Sunday morning, and because my cousin was going to be there, I was excited to accept. From the very first time I attended, I was instantly hooked by the feeling of belonging. I began to go every Sunday I could, and I begged my mom to take me when my aunt and uncle couldn't. Due to my consistent zeal, my uncle bought me my first Bible. I cherished my Bible like it was a bar of pure, solid gold. Except on the very first day I had it, I left it outside in the rain, which left the pages stuck together, the words blurred, and the hardcover wilted. I know it seemed to my uncle I didn't care about the gift he had given me. In reality, I just hated to part with it for one second, even while we were outside playing. When a sudden storm hit in the middle of the day, I bolted inside, leaving my Bible outside. When I remembered, it was too late.

I read my Bible to the best of my elementary-aged ability, and I volunteered with anything I could on Sundays. It was a very small church, so the Sunday school class did not have many kids. As a result, all of the children who attended became my best friends, and the teachers became my role models. They were the first good role models, outside of my family, I ever had. They taught me about God, but even more than teaching me, I saw how they lived their lives. They lived to serve others, and they looked so happy, fulfilled, and at peace.

Going to church felt like an escape. When home life was chaotic, this was my place of refuge and calm. My mom was trying to pick herself up from the mess of leaving Scott, her father dying, moving us, dating again, and meeting Brandon. My mom was single, hard-working, and extremely busy. Homelife got lonely being an only child to a busy mom. Going to church was the cure to my loneliness, and learning about Jesus gave my life meaning.

The more I learned, the more ready I became to move forward with my faith. It was a spring Sunday morning as I sat in the front row of the church, waiting patiently for my turn to talk to the pastor. I was a baby at six years old, but I bravely sat there pressing out the wrinkles of my white flowing dress. When he finished up service, I walked up to the pastor, with trembling hands, clutching onto my wilted Bible for dear life. "Pastor Tommy, I want to be baptized." I didn't exactly know what it meant at the time, but I knew it was a step you should take if you wanted to commit your life to Jesus. He sat down with me and described exactly what it meant to be baptized. I knew I was ready. I wanted a public declaration of who I was becoming and how I wanted to live my life from there on out. I wanted my sins, as small as they were, to be washed clean. A few weekends later, the entire church met at the dark brown, murky waters of the intracoastal waterway. Not exactly where I pictured getting washed clean of my sins, but nonetheless, I was ready to take this step. I was nervous, but I walked into the water where Pastor Tommy was, and a crowd of people gathered around me.

"Riki-Leigh, is Jesus Christ your Lord and Savior?"

I tremblingly replied, "Yes Sir."

"Ok. Then in obedience to our Lord and Savior Jesus Christ, and upon your profession of faith, I baptize you, my sister, in the name of the Father, Son, and Holy Spirit. Amen."

I came up out of the water and felt new. I really did. I had never done anything besides sit in Sunday School. That day I confessed in front of everyone my life belonged to someone and something much bigger than myself. From that point on, my life really did change.

As the years passed, my faith grew exponentially.

When my aunt and uncle transitioned to another church many years later, I was nervous, but it didn't change the path I was on. My faith became a personal journey, extending far beyond a church setting. The next chapter of my walk began as my life at home was becoming a new kind of chaotic. Brandon had left my mom, so her downward spiral with addiction was beginning and growing. I once again needed the community of church as my place of escape. If I had a ride and the doors were open, I was at church. I submersed myself in youth group, Sunday service, Bible studies, and out-of-town conferences. I met friends and found accountability. That is when I truly started loving Christianity as a whole and understanding the parts that were incomprehensible when I was a child.

It wasn't about following rules or sitting nice and pretty for this King in Heaven. It became about loving my Creator, not because I had to *but because I wanted to*. Because I was thankful for this life and thankful I could mess up a thousand times and still be considered worthy to Him. It became about loving others, no matter how different they were from me. It became about living my life to a certain standard, not because someone told me to, but because I wanted to "be the light of the world." I wanted to live my life in such a way that when people looked at me, they saw exactly what I saw in my first role models: happiness, fulfillment, and peace. I wanted people to ask me how I could find those things in the midst of a painful life, and I wanted to be able to BOLDLY tell them it was all because of God. I wanted to say my faith had changed *everything*.

I found ways to tell people about my faith every chance I got. I walked around on the playground and spread the Word like I was an itinerant preacher. I wanted people to understand how my life changed. My youth pastor knew I enjoyed telling people little stories about miracles, faith, etcetera, so he asked me to share one of my examples with my youth group. It was a short story about how I wanted to go to church but didn't have a ride. I prayed I would find a way to go, and right after I prayed that specific prayer, my aunt called and said she was on the way to church if I wanted to go. It was a five-minute story, but I was excited they had asked me to speak, so I invited all of my friends to join me that night.

What I know now, that I didn't have a clue about then, is that two of the people I invited wouldn't live to see 25 years old. One of them wouldn't even live to see 16 years old. While they were both wonderful people, and I don't think that particular night changed anything in their hearts about who Jesus was, I look back and at least know for certain, on that night, they saw the love of Jesus because I was bold enough to share my faith as a teenager. That gives me encouragement as an adult to keep it up and share my story, even though it seems scary at times.

As the years went by, I fell out of the church scene time and time again. When my mom was lost in addiction, I was a teenager and had access to vehicles. I could technically get to church whenever I wanted now because I had my own transportation. But I also had more access to a free life, and getting out of my house meant spending more time with my friends. I had an on-and-off momentum with church. My faith was still there, but I wasn't as eager to regularly attend church. Because I didn't attend and surround myself with people of similar faith and boldness, I wasn't as eager to share my faith stories with others around me as often as I once did.

When I moved away to college, I longed to have a piece of my life at home back. Even though I was in a new city and didn't know a single person who went to church, I scoured the campus for Bible studies. I found one and joined, feeling like a tiny part of what was missing had fallen back into place. We met once a week in the dorm lobby. There were only five of us who attended, but it was what I needed to feel in fellowship with people who shared my same beliefs and helped propel my faith forward. But even as much as I enjoyed it, and my faith was growing, it was challenging to make a weekly Bible study a regular part of my college life. I somehow fit in the parties and pint nights, but Bible study seemed like too much of a commitment.

I wanted my two worlds to fuse, but I didn't exactly know how to fit those pieces together. I wanted to party with my friends and live the college experience, but I also needed to be grounded in my religion, purpose, and the foundation of who I was. The tension in trying to choose which route to take was an internal battle I fought for a long time before I decided Bible study was too cumbersome. I had a lot of studying that needed to be done, and the weekends were filled with games and parties. I told myself I was young and would get back into it eventually.

That night, at nineteen years old, when I decided to quit Bible study because I was "young and would get back into it," I made two decisions I didn't realize I was making at the time. It was essentially the same decision played out in two opposite ways at the same moment. First, I knew religion was important to me, and I needed it to be a major part of my life. I knew it was the foundation of my past and of my future, and I was acknowledging, without it, I wouldn't be the person I was truly meant to be. I told myself that night, as I was quitting, I would find my way back to it. It was a promise I knew I would keep.

The second decision I made that night is a bit trickier

and more infused with immaturity and lack of wisdom. Even though I was deciding that night my religion was the foundation for my life, I was ultimately deciding it didn't fit into my present. It didn't match the life I wanted to live at the time. I often wonder how my life would have played out over the next decade when things got rocky if I had chosen to stick it out and hold tight to my religion. I wonder if I would have had the strength to choose Godly promises over worldly desires. I wonder if I would've found joy in times of suffering. Would I have crumbled so badly when my grandma died years later? Would I have made better decisions in the coming years?

Everyone experiences faith differently. Some people seek out a Savior to pull them out of their rut when times are bad. Some people try to wait until their lives are in order—only then do they feel worthy enough to enter a church building. Some people are searching for meaning in a very confusing world. I seem to need my life in order before I go to church because the shame feels too heavy. I often let myself dwell in a place of shame if I am making decisions I know aren't the best for my life. When I am living in shame, I feel like I can't get close to God, to His church, or to the world that desperately needs Him. As much as I hate to admit it, my external circumstances have played a huge role in my walk with the Lord. This is something I am actively trying to break free from, but the devil knows how I work, and he does anything in his power to pull me away.

The next ten years, in regards to my faith, were a roller coaster in every single aspect. The college party lifestyle came to a screeching halt when I got pregnant with my son two years later. But when I left that lifestyle, it opened a door to my heart I had closed. Religion fit in with my new life because I wasn't holding deep shame about who I was versus what I believed in. I had a family, and there wasn't partying on the weekends, so I could welcome God into my mix again. If you are reading this and think it sounds so superficial, it absolutely was. With humanity, it is almost inconceivable to be forgiven and sinful simultaneously. As humans, we often can't initiate forgiveness without change. God doesn't work on human standards. Forgiveness is free to all, at all times. I didn't understand that then. I knew deep in my soul I wanted to wholeheartedly serve God, but I knew I would fall short from time to time. I also knew I would experience pain and hurt if I truly lived the life I was created for and the life that was fully based on the foundation of my faith.

For me, the logical thing to do was to live my life right next to my foundation instead of on it. If things got rough, I told myself I could jump on and would have safety. But, I didn't want to build my life *completely* on a godly foundation; I felt it could all come toppling down if I messed up. I falsely believed I was in control of everything. However, through those years, moments arose in which I had to rush back to the foundation because God and my faith would be the only things that could fully hold me together.

When my grandma was dying of cancer, my foundation of faith felt like the only thing I had. The funny thing about life is when it seemingly feels like everything has been stripped from us, we see what is most important. There wasn't an option to step off of my foundation because my foundation was all I had. Because of that, I found my true purpose during that time. My purpose for that season was to care for her and to extend a Godly love to her and my family. It was crystal clear to me. Because I understood my purpose and how time-sensitive it was, I was able to live it out. I leaned into the Lord and found comfort and refuge, and I brought these to my grandma and my family at a time when we thought they were unattainable. I embraced the pain and suffering because I knew there was a Savior on the other side welcoming my grandma home. But a short while later, after she was gone and the pain of her loss was settling in, with stress piling on, I started turning to new things as comfort and forgot my ultimate purpose: to serve God. Even though I knew God was my surest foundation, it seemed less painful to turn to the world for relief. Alcohol became my comfort, and it had immediate gratification with intense backlash. I didn't have to feel all of the pain, but I wasn't able to live out my purpose. Knowing I wasn't living out my purpose allowed for shame to enter the picture again.

Shame is a simple word for not feeling enough. It leaves you feeling worthless, powerless, and inept. Shame crept into my mind many times, and when I allowed myself to wallow in it, I immediately stepped off of a godly foundation. Shame throws me into the pits of the world where grief and sorrow are always waiting. There has been nothing easy or steady in my walk with God, but the decisions I made at six and nineteen forever shifted how I would navigate my comebacks in life. It doesn't matter how often or how far I fall from my foundation; it still stands firm. It isn't movable because I know what my purpose and values in life are. It doesn't matter what I do or how far I seem off course, it is still right there, ready for me to step on when I need steady ground. My faith gave me purpose and gave me the foundation I will continue to build my life on.

Why Does This Even Matter?

There was a time I had no idea what my purpose in life was. I had faith in God, but I didn't really understand that faith and purpose went hand in hand. I thought faith was believing there was a God and doing what was right, and the purpose was to do something good for the world. A wise person would realize those things are essential to one another. As an adolescent though, I thought they were all separate entities.

Growing up, I had always been told college was my goal in life. Just go to college, get a good job, and then I would be considered successful. Not successful in the monetary kind of way, but successful in the way that I could use my skills to help someone and also provide for my family. At 24, I accomplished that. I had worked so hard in high school and college and was so proud the day I was handed my diploma. I was even more proud the day I got my first check as a pharmacist. I had "made it." I had achieved my goal. After about a year, I felt restless and didn't know why. I was working hard, but I felt empty inside. I realized my career helped me provide for my family, but I wasn't in a position to also fully connect with people the way I felt God leading me. Some people have careers that are also answering God's calling for their lives. I did not. I felt like I had more work to do outside of my career to fulfill my purpose in life.

Christian or not, we should all be living life with purpose. When the Pharisees asked Jesus which commandment was the greatest, he replied: "Love the Lord your God with all your heart and with all your soul and with all your mind…. and the second is like it: "love your neighbor as yourself" (Matthew 22:37-39, NIV). Those two commandments alone cover everything we need to know about building our foundation and finding our purpose. If you consider your faith to be your foundation, faith is demonstrated by loving God with all your heart, soul, and mind. Building your life on top of that foundation means to live with purpose. If you are stuck finding your purpose in this world, I would love to suggest a single way to find it: that second greatest commandment, *Love your neighbor as yourself.* Do that, and see where it leads you.

As we navigate through this chapter, I want you to understand how essential finding your foundation and purpose is for your life. Knowing what my foundation in life is and the purpose I have that allows me to build onto that foundation is essential to who I am as a person. We are human, and we sin. I know sin taunts me on the daily. I am easily led astray. My only hope to not fall into the trenches of sin and shame is to keep firm on my foundation and to keep my purpose fresh in my mind. I know many people struggle in life with this. I read a scary statistic. In 2017, 47,173 people in the United States completed suicide.[2] That statistic is heart wrenching. I know there are so many factors including mental illness and trauma that play a role in the brutal decision to end one's own life. However, I have to wonder if some of those beautiful souls needed guidance to realize their foundation and purpose in this life.

When you can define your foundation and use it to live out your purpose, you *know without a doubt* your life on Earth is meaningful and essential. There is no option to intentionally leave this Earth because you have a purpose to fulfill. You have work to do. You know you have lives to change. You know this world is better because you are in it. There are so many ways the world can try to blind us to that and rob us of seeing the purpose we have. I am here to tell you that if you stand firm on your foundation, you will be able to see right through those blinders. You will see that your life matters, despite what anyone or anything has you believing.

Now, let's dive into our life application for this chapter:

Here is your life application:

Step 1: Identify your foundation.

My foundation is rooted in my Christian belief that Jesus was crucified for our sins, and when I believe that and follow Him, I will have a place in eternity. My faith is my foundation because it doesn't change over time. God is a constant. His promise is a constant. I may change. There may be seasons of my life when I reorder my priorities, but my faith is still rooted in God's promise. If you are a Christian, then your foundation *has* to be your faith. The Bible says, "For no one can lay any foundation other than the one already laid, which is Jesus Christ" (1 Corinthians 3:11, NIV). It is the only thing that keeps us fighting the good fight and obeying the two greatest commandments given to us by Jesus. It is the only way to fight off sin daily. Claim it today, and stand firm knowing that your foundation will never fail because God never fails.

If you are unsure of your faith at this stage in your life, then I encourage you to find a quality that you want to possess. Do a quick google search of "core values" to find which values stick out to you as essential to your life. Core values are basically life skill words. If you never thought about your core values, it could be a little confusing at first because all of the characteristics seem suitable for a productive lifestyle. Even though they are all great values to have, not all of them resonate to us as critical for *our lives*. These are words like growth, peace, integrity, authenticity, honesty, faith, happiness, love, leadership, self-respect, stability, success, etc. When first reading a core value list, I know you ideally want all of these values in your life because they are great qualities. But when looking at them, pick out 3-5 that truly stand out as values that you can't live without; without that single quality, you would feel empty.

I have made several core value lists I believe are essential to me, my marriage, and our family. While my faith is my foundation, my core value list helps me stay focused on what truly matters in my life. If faith isn't your foundation, use one of these words to guide who you are as a person. These qualities don't change over time. They will be a constant in your ever-evolving life. They will guide you in every decision you make. If you choose "integrity" or "authenticity" as your word, for every decision you make, ask yourself if it aligns with your values. "Am I doing this with integrity? Am I being true to myself, or authentic, by going to this party tonight?" These words become the foundation of your decision-making process and ultimately shape how you live your life.

Step 2: Use your foundation to find your purpose.

I've heard the quote my entire life, "As long as you are breathing, you still have a purpose." Upon hearing this, I would half nod my head, thinking the quote was probably right to some degree, but I also questioned what that means for the lives that ended too soon. Had they fulfilled their purpose so much sooner than the rest of us? Did they have some divine way of knowing they only had a short time to complete their task? It wasn't until recently that I considered my scope of thinking was for a human mind, seeing only through the lens of a lifetime rather than eternity. As humans, we don't naturally know our purpose, but "it is God who works in you to will and to act in order to fulfill his good purpose" (Philippians 2:13, NIV). In some way, that can give us all relief.

If you are like me, you probably like to have a plan and chase after your goal, your purpose being no different. But a purpose for your entire life is a daunting task. We have one life to live. How do we use that little bit of time to change the world? I instantly think of Mother Theresa, Martin Luther King Jr., Beth Moore, Harriet Tubman, and even Angelina Jolie. They have used their time to try consistently and passionately to make the world a better place, all in different ways. I see them, and I am in awe of their diligence but am often left hopeless for my own place in that. How does an average woman, with a job and kids, pursue changing the world or have an audience large enough to actually make a change?

I know some people do make it happen, but recently, I have instead decided to rely on Philippians 2:13, for my strength. If I, or you, or anyone else, has Christ in their heart, then it is by Him working in you and through you that your purpose in life may be fulfilled. If we decide to lean not on our own understanding, our own audience, or our own ideas to fulfill our destiny, and instead choose to trust that God works in ways beyond our earthly understanding, then our purpose will be fulfilled in bold ways.

So what exactly does that mean for the planner and the task-oriented person? To just sit back and trust that God is actively working miracles to save the world through us? For me, no. The Bible is our training manual in all situations. Even if we have faith that God is working within us to complete our purpose, we can still use our manual to see how to live out that faith.

"What good is it, my brothers and sisters, if someone claims to have faith but has no deeds? Can such faith save them? Suppose a brother or a sister is without clothes and daily food. If one of you says to them, "Go in peace; keep warm and well fed," but does nothing about their physical needs, what good is it?

*In the same way, faith by itself, if it is not
accompanied by action, is dead."*
(James 2: 14-17, NIV)

The entire book of James is an instruction manual on how to live a Godly life, and I find myself going back to it time and time again for answers. We already know from Philippians, that God works through us to fulfill his purpose, and in James, we see that faith and deeds go hand in hand. Even though we are given very specific instructions, I need even more. What kind of deeds does James mean? That's when I go back to that second greatest commandment given by Jesus: *"Love your neighbor as yourself."* Start there.

Step 3: Using your purpose to change your life.

By simply loving your neighbor as yourself, you can single-handedly change your life, change the world, and fulfill your purpose. It seems easy and thrilling to accomplish so much with one small step. This is a life-changing step. However, most people find it hard to start here. Why? Because this step is unglamorous. It doesn't come with recognition or fame at the end. So many of us want our seal of approval after we do something good: the picture of us with orphans on our mission trip, the thank you from the person you just bought food for, the big bag of trash after the beach cleanup. Something tangible that screams, "I did something good!". Even though these things give us the rush of dopamine (our feel-good hormone), nothing is as impactful as the small waves you make inside of the walls of your own home. Start with your family. When I was at rock-bottom in my life, the only thing I felt like I had was my faith and purpose. At first, I felt discouraged because I was in a place I couldn't see outside of the depression I was in to figure out a way to change the world through loving others. That's when I realized I needed to focus on the people in my home first.

Love your spouse, love your parents, love your children. It may not look like much at first, but there is a generational impact in raising your kids up to know eternal love. Think of God's promise to Abraham. He was promised his descendants would be as numerous as the stars in the sky, yet he only had one son through his wife at the time. Loving your family teaches them to love their family one day, and they will teach their family to love their family for generations to come. Love your family, and see the world change. Maybe not today or tomorrow or in your lifetime, but the generational impact is everlasting.

It doesn't have to stop with your family, though. Loving others can manifest into anything: feeding the homeless, advocating for the oppressed, helping storm-ravaged towns, etc. Letting love lead changes lives, no matter what angle you take.

The hard part of loving others as yourself begins when "the others" aren't like you. Jesus doesn't command us to love the neighbors that look like us, act like us, vote like us, treat others the same as us, or have the same sexual orientation. I know; deep down, we all know that, but it can be daunting at times. How do we love a hateful person? How do we love people that directly go against our beliefs that we believe are *good*? I think that's where people get too caught up in being right and changing someone and lose sight of the commandment to "love your neighbor as yourself."

When you show love without question, even to those filled with hate and sin, the world sees that. The hateful person sees that. You may not notice a change immediately, or even in your lifetime, but your love will change people. Love is like a light. If you are in a dark room and one person needs to see, you help by shining a flashlight for them. You may be shining the light to help that *one* person to see, but everyone around will also see the light just because they are close. Love works in the same way. Everyone around will see. Be the example of love to the world, and be the light for all to see.

Step 4: How to use your foundation when you fail.

There are days when I fail. There are days when love doesn't win. There are days I haven't loved my neighbor, my family, or myself. I am here to tell you it happens to every single one of us. As much as I love telling readers that *you can change the world*, I equally want to tell you it is okay to feel like you failed. That is why it is so important to know what your foundation is. If your foundation rests in God, then nothing can take that from you. Not one mistake or a million disappointments.

Our faith gives us hope that our slates were washed clean on the day Jesus died on the cross for us, and because of that, grace is extended to us on all days we feel like a failure. Romans 8:28, NKJV, says, "And we know that all things work together for good to those who love God, to those who are called according to *His* purpose." God works through all situations to fulfill His purpose. Whether you feel like you are killing it in this life, changing lives and loving everyone you can, or whether you are struggling to even get out of bed, if you know your foundation is unshakeable, you have a safe place to fall. Life is hard. There is sin, failure, sickness, and violence, but you were put on this Earth for good reasons. God will work through you to raise you up through hardships and through victories to fulfill His eternal purpose.

Four

ACCEPTING THE TRANSITION

After my boyfriend broke up with me, I was lucky enough to have friends that came rushing in to pick me up. I didn't deserve it, and I didn't expect it to happen. I thought I would be left without anyone: parents, boyfriend, or friends. Instead, they kept me busy. Even as I cried in the car on the way to places, they were there to hold my hand through it. At first, I still felt lonely and out of place. But over time, I started enjoying it. I'd missed girl time.

The problem with my new situation after my boyfriend broke up with me was that I never found self-worth. I replaced my boyfriend with my friends. While I used to look at him and how much he loved me for assurance, my worth was now wrapped up in how I was fitting in with my friends. I was always anxious and checking in with people to see what they were doing, and I was worried I was going to be left out in some way. I said *yes* to things I didn't care about to get approval from people who loved me regardless. I never even asked my friends if they cared if I didn't attend something. I assumed if I wasn't in the middle of a hangout, then they would forget about me.

Those last years of high school were filled with so many *yeses* I couldn't keep count. Don't be mistaken, I enjoyed most of the things I went to. But somewhere, I lost who I was as a person. I thought I had to be at everything to have friends or to be considered popular or worthy. My mom was still non-existent during this time, so I had the freedom to do what I wanted. If I wasn't at a party, then I was hosting a party. There is no pause in life when you live it to impress other people. The mentality of living to impress other people was evident in my life. I signed up for every club and after-school activity I could. I was stretched thin and anxious, but in my mind, I felt fulfilled. I was filling the void of heartbreak and loneliness, and if I wasn't hurting anymore, I considered it to be a good thing.

When college admissions became the topic of conversation, everyone around me was so excited. There was a lot of anticipation for the next big step in our lives. My friends were talking about moving to new cities and meeting new friends like their world was about to get ten times better than it had ever been. They were getting ready to start a whole new life, and they thought that was the greatest thing in the world.

I wasn't excited. I did what I was supposed to do, and I applied to all kinds of schools. But I had a pit in my stomach for a year leading up to graduation. I did not want to start a new life. I did not want to make new friends. I had just invested all of my time and energy into proving myself worthy enough to have the friends I had. My friends were the entire reason I felt loved and wanted. Moving to a new place to meet new friends honestly seemed like torture.

When the time came to pick out the college and city of my dreams, I went with the obvious pick. Not the one in the big city, or the one with the prettiest scenery, or the one with the best football team or academic performance…Instead, I chose the one my best friend was going to. Not only would we go to the same school, but we would share a dorm room together.

It seemed like such an obvious thing to do at the time, even though people warned us not to do it. They said we needed to meet new people and learn independence. She was a social butterfly and already so independent, so I am still confused as to why she was so on board with it. I knew why I wanted to do it. I needed someone. Because without someone beside me, I didn't feel like a whole person.

From the moment I stepped foot on our college campus, I felt like an alien. I never felt like I belonged. There were so many people, and there was so much to do. I didn't know how to make friends because the classes were huge, and once I met someone during one class, I couldn't find them for the next one. The partying that started in high school only intensified in college. I tried so hard to put on a happy face. I did everything in my power to make good grades, be involved in clubs, to meet new friends, and find them again so they actually became friends. I felt what I was doing was unsustainable and impossible, yet, everyone I looked at seemed to be doing it with ease.

I was living in a world where everyone seemed to be independently living their lives, forgetting about the past, and working toward a beautiful future. I desperately wanted that for myself, too. I did the things. I joined the clubs, laughed with my friends, and partied until the wee hours of the morning. The experiences I had there are irreplaceable, beautiful memories I treasure greatly, but no matter the fun I was having or the memories I was making, I missed the comfort of home and the comfort of my old friends. The weirdest thing about being away at college was desperately missing home but realizing I didn't have anything there to miss. Everything I loved was gone. My grandma sold the house my mom and I lived in on the day I left for college, so I didn't even have a home to come back to.

Since I couldn't physically return home, I stayed in constant contact with most of my good friends from high school. Over time the number shrank, but a close circle of us never lost contact. I thought that through this experience, I would learn independence or how to find worth in myself alone, but I didn't. I just clung stronger to my small circle of people.

Having people come and visit us was one of my favorite parts of college. The feeling of having our dorm filled with people from home, in my new town, in my very own dorm room, made me feel so grown up and gave me the comfort of home. My very best friend from high school and two of our guy friends were visiting almost every weekend. One of those friends was Andy.

Andy and I were in the same friend circle throughout high school, but we never had pushed the friendship boundary. I wasn't really interested in dating anyone after my breakup, and he was either dating or interested in other girls from our friend circle. But I considered him a friend. As our first year of college wrapped up, Andy came to visit enough times that I was finally open to the idea of dating again. Andy liked to party, which was pretty much a requirement if you were visiting our college. But he also liked movie nights with his family, and he had very involved parents, compared to my mom who gave me complete freedom. That's what drew me to him. He was a nice mix of a bad boy with good family life— something that I wanted. When I returned to my grandma's house for the summer, the two of us started dating. We had no idea if it would be a summer fling or something much more, but we were open to the idea of anything.

During our first summer together, we were together

constantly. He consumed every single day of my summer, and I loved it. We spent our time focusing on having fun and getting to know each other. I soaked up our days together, hoping time would slow down for me and my summer romance. But as quickly as it came, summer ended just as fast, and I knew I had to move back to college and leave this behind. It was a real internal battle deciding how I was going to navigate this new relationship I had with Andy, keeping up this lifestyle I had at school. It was difficult to return to the hustle of school after such a slow summer at home; one that was primarily focused on my growing relationship.

I returned to this big city, a new apartment, and a huge load of classes. That alone seemed overwhelming, but I also had a boyfriend back at home, who I was supposed to be, at the very least, calling to talk to every night. Within just a few weeks, it felt impossible to navigate my college world and my relationship. They felt like polar opposites. During the weekends when Andy came to my town, we shut the world out so we could enjoy our time together. But when I was alone at school, he always came last on the priority list. At that time, and for many years, he took it personally. He thought it was something lacking in our relationship, and he desperately tried to fix a problem that was impossible to fix. I was stuck in the middle of two worlds, unable to find the balance between the two.

Even though our relationship was hard, I didn't want to lose him at all. We stuck it out throughout the next two years of long-distance. When I returned to school after our second summer together, I thought the transition was going to be easier. Instead, it was even harder. I finally found my niche at college and had a solid group of friends. There were two girls I was close with who were also in serious long-distance relationships. I always stuck with them when we went out, and because of them, my relationship became easier.

I still cared deeply about what other people thought of me, and I did not want to be the only person I knew in a serious relationship. Having two friends in the same boat as I felt safe. I stuck with them during our nights out, and I always felt like even though most people weren't in a relationship, at least they were by my side. Sometime during that second season of long-distance dating, that comfort of having friends who understood came crashing down when both of my friends decided to end their relationships. It is doubtful anyone ever knew how much these two breakups, which literally had nothing to do with me, affected me. I knew what they were doing was best for them, but it felt like a personal attack on my relationship.

Andy and I were not breaking up; in fact, we were getting closer every day. By now I knew I loved him and could see a future with him…but the thought of me being the only person I knew in a relationship was unbearable. I didn't go out five nights a week like a lot of people, but I went out often. Andy was already frustrated with the lack of time we got together. Now that I didn't have a single friend who was in a committed relationship, it was harder for me to juggle friendships and my relationship. We started arguing a lot, and there was one time I flat out broke up with him. I even made it official on Facebook. This game of keeping up with everyone else and keeping up with him, three hours away, was too much for me to take on. I really *did* want it to end. I needed the balancing game to end.

I was so tired of the weekend traveling and feeling left out. I felt like the odd man out every day of my life, and I truly hated it. I wanted to focus on myself. However, our breakup was short-lived. Just a week after I broke up with him, he asked if he could travel up to see me for Valentine's Day.

As soon as I saw him, I knew I had to make this work. I knew he would one day be my husband. I just still had a hard time grasping that my future was starting many years before I had envisioned it. I was only 20 years old when I knew I would be with this guy for the rest of my life. It seemed inconceivable.

Even though I knew he was my future, I was still determined to be *both* a college girl and a committed girlfriend. A month went by and things felt good between us. It was exam time, so I wasn't going out as much. I spent more time talking to Andy and could give our relationship the attention it needed. I wasn't even worried about missing out on fun events with my friends because right after exams were over, my friends and I had planned a trip to Panama City, Florida, for spring break! Andy was fearful over the trip because he thought college spring breaks were wild (He was right).

As the exam week passed, and the trip was coming up, I was getting fearful about something else. Something big—something that would be very unexpected and change the course of my life forever. I kept my worries to myself, but every day, I was checking my calendar and calculating dates. Did I really miss a period or did I forget to write down the last one I had? I was refusing to let myself worry about something like this. I knew I was overreacting. I had only seen Andy once in the past three months, so the possibility of getting pregnant that weekend was super slim…right?

I went to Panama City with my group of closest girlfriends and had the time of my life. The beach was beautiful, it was so hot out, and there were concerts on the beach all week long. We were in the front row at a beach concert hanging out with Nicki Minaj, Lil Wayne, and Kid Cudi, having an unforgettable experience. However, when the concert was over, the sun had set, and all of my friends were sleeping, I was still awake. I was laying on the bed googling pregnancy symptoms, trying to ignore the pain I was having in my stomach. I still didn't tell anyone. I just told myself as soon as we got home, I would take a pregnancy test.

The morning after we returned from our spring break trip, I stumbled to the bathroom, excited to put my mind at ease. I knew I was overreacting, and there was an explanation for this. Two minutes later, I peeked at the test to find out my fate…and what I saw was definitely an explanation for all of my symptoms, but not the explanation I was hoping for. I was pregnant.

I woke up all of my roommates with my hysterical sobs. I couldn't hold it together. This could not be my reality. I cried until I couldn't cry anymore, and then I threw up. I couldn't have picked worse timing because that day I had to work a double. I spent the next twelve hours being a waitress and putting a smile on my face, all while freaking out inside. I called Andy on the way to work that morning to tell him, and he immediately drove the three hours to be with me.

When I got home from work I continued to puke. Between the toilet visits, we talked about our future. When I talked about what we would do, I was panicking. I was in college. I needed to graduate. I lived with my friends. I had no money! It was all focused on the situation we were in at the moment. When Andy voiced what he was feeling, all he said was that we would make it work, and we would be a family. His naive optimism made me enraged. How could he sit and think about the future when this is happening RIGHT NOW? This couldn't work. I could not bring a baby into the world I was living in right now.

Our conflicting feelings about this situation only made one thing clear to me. I couldn't be honest with him anymore.

He didn't fear any of my fears. He wasn't realistically problem-solving; he was just telling me it would be okay. When I told more of my friends and even some family, I was met with a wide range of reactions. My best friend that often came to visit, immediately told me that I could do this and overnighted a box of parenting books. Other people told me I should have an abortion. But mostly, people were right in the middle.

All these reactions did for me was confuse me to no end. During the day, when I was at class or with my friends, I thought the answer was abortion. I couldn't envision bringing a baby into the world I was living in. It wasn't that I didn't want a baby because I had been waiting my entire life to be a mom. I just didn't want to have a baby suffer because of my instability. I wanted my child to be born into a world with everything I had ever wanted and needed. I didn't want my child to skip lunch because they didn't have lunch money, or never have new clothes, or never see their parents because we would be working two jobs to survive.

I wanted to finish school so I could give the *world* to my baby. If I had a baby then, surely my life would be over. I would have no education, social life, or big plans for the future. Later, when I would lay in bed at night, I forgot about all of that. I envisioned a family, snuggled on the couch while watching movies. Kissing *my* baby. Rocking my baby. Loving my baby. A beautiful growing belly. Literally everything my dreams were made of.

The back and forth in my mind was grueling. I finally decided I couldn't be the one to decide. I needed someone outside of the situation who didn't know they were making a decision for me to be my decision-maker. I had just applied to a doctorate program. If I got in, it seemed impossible to raise a child and go to school. I decided I would wait for one week for my admissions letter. If I didn't get in, I would keep the baby. In the meantime, I would continue to throw up every ten minutes and cry myself to sleep.

During the week-long waiting process, I had a flashback to just a year prior that made me sick to my stomach. I had an assignment for my public speaking class where I had to take one side of a controversial topic and present my case to the class. Do you want to know what I picked? The case AGAINST abortion. I had *always* been against abortion. I enjoyed every minute of making a poster full of mangled fetal body parts, and when it was my turn to present, I presented this topic loud and proud. I told every person how abortion was inhumane and wrong. Now, I was thinking about that speech and asked myself, "Did I ever look up at the people I was talking to? Did I ever take the time to notice if a girl had had her head down, or tears running down her cheeks, or a look of regret on her face?" This is not to say I shouldn't have presented or you shouldn't take the Pro-Life stance. Even now, I would still take that same position and present that poster. You should absolutely fight for what you believe in, and I'm proud I did. But man, I could have done it with compassion. I could have done it with love and understanding. Unknown to me at the time, a year later, I would be that girl. I would be the girl googling images late at night, regretting the decision I had made. I would be the girl forced to wake up every day for the rest of her life asking "what if" or "what would the baby be doing now?" A year later, *I was the girl who made a choice she would regret for the rest of her life.*

The choice I made was the result of desperation. I took myself out of the equation and pretended that the acceptance letter into graduate school was the thing that decided, not me. When the doctor said to me, "If you do this there is no turning back," I didn't allow myself even a second to process those words. I instantly went through with it without questioning my decision. I knew if I thought about it, even for a second, I would change my mind. The irony of the decision I made was that I'd applied to graduate school for *my kids*. I had always wanted to be a mom. I just knew whenever that day came, I wouldn't want my kids to suffer through a life of making ends meet. I wanted them to have a good life. I just had no faith at the time that God makes every situation work out for good, even if it meant being a mom while in school.

No one besides my roommates knew what I did. We said I had an unfortunate accident, and the pregnancy was over. Andy was heartbroken, but again, he immediately came to Columbia to support me. I didn't want any support though. The second I made the decision that I couldn't take back, I changed. I hated myself. I *hated* myself. It was like I had been holding a veil over my eyes for years, and suddenly, it was ripped away. I looked around at the life I was living, and I absolutely abhorred every single thing about it. I hated the late nights. I hated partying. I hated impressing other people. I hated the school clubs I was involved in. I hated the good grades I earned. I hated that I made a permanent decision based on all the temporary things around me. I hated that the biggest dream of my life was in the palm of my hand, and I destroyed it.

No one really asked how I was doing after. I guess they all pretty much thought it was a good thing; that God had decided Himself that the timing was wrong. I knew God didn't make that choice. I did. A choice I deeply regretted. I stopped going to class and secluded myself from most of my friends. I ended up failing two classes that semester when I had never even earned a *C* before. I wanted to desperately turn back time and take it all back, but I couldn't. My heart was broken. From that day forward, I could never and would never be the same girl I was just minutes before I took that pregnancy test. She was long gone.

Even though the old me was gone, the new me was going to rise up stronger and braver than before.

Why Does This Even Matter?

If I am being completely transparent, I was not going to write this chapter. I have never talked about that day. I have tried so hard to forget it, although I could never. The last thing I want to do is to write about it in a book available to anyone in this world. As I got closer and closer to this time of my life in the book-writing process, I could feel God gently nudging me to tell my story. Writing this chapter has been one of my greatest acts of obedience to date. I know God has a plan to use this chapter, despite my utter dread in typing these words. I learned one of the greatest lessons of my entire life when this happened. It just really sucks to write about it.

The day I made that decision, my life changed. The analogy of a veil over my eyes being pulled away describes it exactly. I had no idea I was even living everyone else's life. I thought what I was doing was what had to be done. I honestly thought you had to fit in and do what everyone else did until the acceptable time came to break free and "grow up." When I realized I had made a decision that went against everything I had ever stood for because I didn't "fit in," that's when the veil was pulled away. I realized then, only after it was too late, this was actually *my* life. I could choose what I wanted to do with it.

The lesson I learned was about living your life, even

if it looks different from the life those around you are living. What frustrated me the most was that I'd seen my life shifting for years, but I wouldn't let myself accept it. As Andy and I got closer, I knew he would be my husband. It took me a while to realize that, but even when I realized it, I still wouldn't let myself accept it. My plan didn't look like everyone else's plan, and I did not like that. Therefore, I wouldn't let myself live it out.

Before I get started talking about the steps to accepting when a transition is happening in your life, I want you to realize what I am NOT saying. I am not saying jump headfirst into a relationship and leave your friendships in the dust when you fall in love at eighteen years old or at any age. Definitely, protect yourself and your future. I can applaud myself for having boundaries at eighteen years old, even if they were faulty. When my daughters are eighteen, I will probably tell them to do exactly what I did—live your best life, put friends and school first, and don't worry about the boyfriend because if he loves you, then he will stick around. I just hope maybe my daughters will be more honest with themselves and those around them about their situation. I hope they go to the Truth and get wisdom from God first, before consulting with anyone else.

I should have been honest with those around me about my conflicting feelings. I didn't let anyone into the thoughts running through my mind. I wanted both. I wanted friends, college life, and a serious boyfriend. The anxiety wasn't necessary if I would have just been honest with myself and others about my feelings. There were other people with serious boyfriends in college still enjoying their lives because they found balance and were upfront with everyone around them.

Now that you know what I am *not* saying, let's dive

into what I *am* saying. This is what I needed to hear at twenty years old, but I also needed to hear this at fifteen and thirty, and probably when I am fifty years old too. It is so applicable to every stage of life. I know we are all focused on our present situations. We are constantly focused on our daily to-do lists and our current problems, and we put so much effort into those "now" types of things. I do feel that is a good quality in a lot of ways. That is how we get through our lives—by staying constantly aware of what is happening around us so we can tackle the daily problems. But every so often, we have to start looking at the future. We must do this if we want our futures to look any different than what our current lives look like.

Here is your life application for this chapter:

Step 1: Envision your future in five years. Five years only. Anything longer than that is too far in the future, and so much could change in that time. A year is way too short and flies by in the blink of an eye. But in five years, what do you want your life to look like? Ask yourself these questions, and write out the answers. If I focus on making my dreams a reality, what does my life in five years consist of? What does my family look like? What does my faith look like? What job do I have? Am I dating, married, single? Do I have kids? Have I traveled? Have I finished school? What am I doing in my free time? Who are my friends? What do I do when I see my friends? Am I happy? (I hope that is a *yes* since this is your ideal life.) What am I doing to stay happy?

Now that you have written this down, do you see a big difference between where you are right now and where you want to be in five years? If that answer is *yes*, then you have work to do. Five years go by so unbelievably fast. You do not want to look at your life in five years and see nothing has changed except the year. I have done that. I thought I would be in a completely different place once five years had passed. Except I did nothing to get myself there, and I ended up looking, when time passed, and realizing the only thing that had changed was my age. I was in the exact same spot—still with the same goals, but not an inch closer to any of them. The feelings I got when I realized this were disappointment and shame. Things happen that prevent you from reaching all your goals, and that is totally okay. Give yourself grace. But what isn't okay is having a dream for your life and refusing to make daily moves to get there. Even tiny moves add up in five years.

When I was nineteen, I should have looked at where I wanted to be in five years. I needed to look beyond the life I was living day-to-day. I had always envisioned myself getting married and starting a family young. That was the dream of my life. I wanted dinner dates with friends and quiet nights at home. If I'd looked at my future, I would have still seen myself in graduate school but with a little family by my side. I didn't see traveling the world (at least not in five years) or climbing the corporate ladder to be a CEO like most of my friends. Their present-day lifestyle, for most of them, aligned perfectly with where they saw themselves in five years. Mine didn't. If only I would have looked just a little outside of my box of the present, I would have seen that my vision of life in five years would require me to make changes to get there. I would have let myself live out some of my dreams. I would have given myself permission to step away from everyone else's dream to live my own.

It still makes me sad to know I gave up a dream when it was there, literally happening within me, and I wouldn't let myself take hold of it. That is something I will live with forever, and I think about it so often. But one thing that changed from that decision I made was I would never get so lost in the here and now that I couldn't see a future.

Step 2: Make specific goals based on your five-year dreams. I separate my goals into five categories, mostly because I am Type A, but also because I like to have a plan of action. If you aren't planning for a future, then you are ultimately planning for things to stay the same. Typically, my goals fall into these five categories: Health, Faith, Family, Career, Fun. Having categories breaks down your dreams to tangible goals, rather than having a giant list of things you should change. First, create your categories. You can come up with your own or use mine. Then, using your five-year dreams, write down your five-year goals for each category. Here are a few examples of five-year goals:

These would have been my nineteen-year-old, five-year life goals:
- **Health:** Not a fast-food eater. Exercises regularly.
- **Faith:** Be an active member of church. Volunteer regularly.
- **Family:** Get married to Andy, have our own house, have a baby.
- **Career:** Graduate from Pharmacy school! Get a job as a pharmacist.

My five-year life goals now:
- **Health:** Be a half-marathon runner. Be in the best shape of my life.
- **Faith:** Create a non-profit that helps families in poverty. Be a true example of a believer in Jesus who walks daily in that truth.

- **Family:** Take a European vacation with my family. Still be best friends and madly in love with my husband. Spend uninterrupted quality time with each of my children regularly.
- **Career:** Be a published author. Have student loans paid off.

Having some type of idea of what you want your life to look like in five years gets your wheels spinning on how to accomplish those dreams and set up your future in the best possible way. If I had made that list at nineteen, I would have seen I was making the right steps for my career, but I wasn't doing anything to achieve any of the other goals for my life. I was actually preventing those other dreams from happening. I didn't know at nineteen I should be thinking about my future. I didn't realize that daily changes transform you into who you will become over time. I honestly thought one day you just wake up a changed person who has accomplished those dreams. I didn't know that taking small steps every single day, starting TODAY, is what it takes to make dreams come to life.

Step 3: Look at your five-year goals and have a "next-step" planned for each of those. You have to start today if you truly want to see your five-year dreams come to life. So, you get to decide right now how you are going to accomplish these goals. A next-step plan is a baby step. It is just one tiny step closer to your dream life. But once you feel comfortable with that tiny change, then you set another tiny next-step goal. If you can consistently do that over the next five years, you will be where you want to be, and you will be so proud of yourself for accomplishing that goal!

Here are examples of next-step plans based on the above goals I have/had set for myself.

Nineteen-year-old me:
- **Health:** Only order salads when eating fast food.
- **Faith:** Research churches in my area. Narrow it down to three to try.
- **Family:** Have a talk with Andy about our future to see if we are on the same page.
- **Career:** Keep studying. Work hard daily.

Me, now:
- **Health:** Follow a running plan. Increase mileage weekly by 10%.
- **Faith:** Volunteer this month with the outreach group at church.
- **Family:** Set aside money weekly for a vacation fund. Spend less time on my phone when at home to engage more with Andy and the kids.
- **Career:** Write 500 words, five times a week.

I hope you see what I mean by next-step planning. Those tiny plans will make the biggest difference in seeing your dreams change into your reality. If you have a big dream that takes priority over the others, then scale back on your next-step planning with your other categories. Make it truly a tiny baby step, while your big goal has a larger step to get there.

That's how it was for me at nineteen. My main priority was graduating from school. I focused daily on that goal and achieving it. I never made a list to prioritize other areas in my life, but if I had, those next-step plans would have been super tiny. My goal wouldn't be running a marathon at that point; it would simply be getting a salad at the fast-food restaurant instead of a burger. It wasn't getting married, but having a talk to make sure we were on the same page. You decide what takes priority and what needs the most time and energy, but still, have your next step planned for every category.

Unexpected things will happen such as pregnancy, sickness, falling in love, or losing a job. Those life events can ultimately flip your present-day circumstances completely around. However, if you have your mind focused on your life in five years, instead of how one thing changes your life *now*, it can help with the sting of change. Looking at how a circumstance changes your life in the present time will seem hard and scary. That was me at nineteen. A pregnancy flipped my world upside down. It changed everything. But gosh, if I could have seen that my life would be just as fruitful and beautiful (actually *more*), then the pain of change would have been a little easier to bear.

Giving it time, and looking at a broader picture, makes your problems seem less daunting and more manageable. If you know what you want your life to look like, you can easily shift some things to make that vision work or create a new vision. If you are actively taking baby steps to achieve a goal, a huge life change can't really change *everything*. You may have to re-adjust and re-prioritize, but you can still have a beautiful life. Just don't ever get so caught up in the temporary circumstances that all you see is now, and you can't accept your transition to your future.

Not everything works out as planned, and that's okay. What isn't okay is never having a plan. What isn't okay is letting the world decide what *your* future looks like. The future is beautiful, and it is in God's hands. In the Bible, God says He has plans for you, "plans to prosper you and not to harm you, plans to give you hope and a future" (Jeremiah 29:11, NIV). Let your future be all God wants for you. To have that, you must accept this time as your transitional time, and be bold enough to take your next baby step to living out the goals for your life. Your future self will thank you. You deserve this.

Five

INTENTIONALLY CHOOSE YOUR ENVIRONMENT

I was twenty years old. I was living with three of my college best friends. I made a decision I hated myself for but one I would have to live with forever. Internally, I had committed to changing who I was, but I had no idea how. I couldn't grasp the concept of changing one thing at a time and taking baby steps to slowly become who I wanted to be. I was immature and honestly thought I was going to wake up and be that new person I was dreaming about. Every day I woke up, I was expecting I would be happy again. I would have forgiven myself, I would have a new dream in my mind that I was ready to chase, I would stop caring what people thought, and it would be my new beginning.

Instead, though, every day, I was waking up in the same dark hole I had been in when I went to bed. I hated myself. I blamed a lot of people around me for a choice that I had made, and when I saw those people carrying on with their normal lives, it gutted me. It was a dark place to be in.

The only thing that changed immediately from my decision was my relationship with Andy. I had no desire to party or go out anymore. I wanted to check out from whatever life I was living and start fresh. The only person I thought I could trust was Andy. He had no idea, but I heavily relied on him to pull me out of this hole. He was coming into town every weekend trying to cheer me up in any way he knew how. I desperately needed that from him, but I also hated it. He still didn't know what I had done, and the guilt of it intensified whenever he was around. I felt like a stranger to myself because I had absolutely no control over what I was feeling at any moment in time.

I couldn't understand the intense mood changes I was experiencing. No one told me I was going to have post-partum hormone changes. Everything was a trigger to me. One minute, I was so excited to be spending the weekend with Andy, enjoying the activity we planned. Then, the next thing I knew, something would trigger me, and I would cry. My sadness would turn into guilt and anger all within minutes. The constant cycle felt like shackles. I desperately wanted to be free and happy, but I couldn't break free, no matter how hard I tried. He could not keep up with my mood swings, but I was so fortunate he stuck with me through it all. He tried everything he could to make me happy. Andy would ask over and over again what exactly would make me happy, but I didn't know the answer. I kept telling him I needed life to change somehow. Something drastic needed to happen. I needed to be pulled away from this life so I could start a new one without caring.

As our two-year anniversary was approaching, we decided a trip away from everyone would bring some calm and distraction to my hurting heart. For the most part, it worked. We got a hotel room in this quiet, mountain lake town. We hiked up the mountainside, rented canoes, skipped rocks in the creek, and enjoyed our time as a couple. Even though my heart was broken, I felt distracted. It was exactly what I needed. On the last day there, as we were paddling in our canoe on an almost empty lake, Andy turned to me and asked me to reach around to the back of the canoe for our lunch box. It took me a minute, but when I grabbed our lunch and turned back to hand it to him, he was no longer sitting there. Instead, he was down on one knee with an open ring box pointed directly at me!

He was terribly nervous and stumbled through a speech about what was happening…as if it wasn't obvious. Of course, I said *yes*. I grabbed his face, and we kissed in the middle of the open lake that felt like it was entirely ours. No one was there to witness or to make it feel weird. It was just him and me. The world felt right for those moments. I admired the ring he had saved up and purchased for me. I loved him on such a deeper level that day too. He wanted to make everything right in my world. He knew my hurt was deep, and he knew I now desperately wanted a family, even though the timing was obviously not ideal. This was his fix and our first very concrete step to a life together and a family of our own. I appreciated and loved his attempt to mend my heartache, but I knew deep down that until I forgave myself, my heart would never heal.

I literally felt like I was floating on clouds for the remainder of the trip and for most of the drive home until I realized what exactly I was coming home to. Suddenly, I felt like someone had unloaded 100 pounds of rocks into the pit of my stomach. I was going back to my apartment, with my three single roommates, at my apartment complex, full of my twenty single college friends that liked to party four nights a week. How was I supposed to walk into my apartment as a newly engaged woman and not feel like an alien? Andy still wasn't living there. He lived three hours away with absolutely no plans to move to Columbia any time soon.

Suddenly, the spiral started again. The same spiral Andy had hoped this trip was going to put to an end. First,

I started to panic. I didn't want to be the odd man out again. Everyone is going to see this ring on my finger and ask questions. Who gets engaged at twenty years old? How do you marry a person who doesn't live close by? How are you going to plan a wedding in graduate school? No one had actually asked me those questions, but that was what I was imagining. Since the day I had received that positive pregnancy test, I had changed. No matter what I did, I would never be that innocent college girl I was months ago. My life had changed, and I felt like a stranger around everyone. I imagined that an engagement ring on my finger would be even more proof I was different than everyone else. Andy would leave and I would be alone.

I was fully into my panic spiral. I looked at Andy and saw he was completely content, and by the looks of it, HAPPY sitting beside me. Suddenly, my panic turned to anger again. How could he do this to me? My heart was broken beyond repair, and he thought a ring was going to fix me? By the looks of it, it fixed him. But my heart was still in pieces. Now, I had a ring to prove I was changed. He was going to drive back home, continue his normal life, still party with his friends, with no new ring on his finger, as if nothing had changed. Because for him, nothing had changed. He replaced the loss of our baby with a fiancé, so now the past was the past.

By the time we got back to my college town, we were in a fight. I was a mess. He took the ring back and left to go home. With him back at home and me alone at college, I realized ring or no ring, I was never going to be the person I was a few months ago. There was nothing I could do to bring me back the carefree girl I once was. I needed to accept it. I needed to decide how I was going to move on.

Weeks turned into months, and there were still many tears and moments of anger I had to work through with everyone. I was angry with myself, mostly, and Andy, but also with friends and family for no reason other than their lives continued on like normal, even though they knew I was hurting. It had been months of waking up every day, crying, and then going to bed crying before I decided I couldn't live this way any longer. I didn't intentionally set out to make a major change; I just set out to find some happiness each day.

During that process of just finding something to be happy about, I also started to make changes I didn't even know I was making. I was starting to gravitate towards people who were more like the people I was or wanted to be. At work, I would spend more time talking to the newlywed, or when I went home to visit Andy, we would hang out with people who were pregnant or had kids already. It was new to me. I had only ever surrounded myself with mostly single college students for as long as I could remember. Even though they were supportive of every change I was making, I didn't fit into *their* mold of how they were living *their* lives, so I thought my choices were wrong.

The people I started to communicate and spend time with weren't even people I intentionally set out to find. I was subconsciously choosing to make new friends with people who gave me permission to be myself. I finally began to see the light again. The crying and emotional outbursts came to an end, and I was growing excited about my and Andy's future together. He eventually gave me my ring back. Our lives were still separate, and it was still hard, but we were committed to figuring it out together.

Getting out of that dark place was a longer process than I like to admit. I felt like a new person. Surrounding myself with people who were living life differently allowed me to do the same. I was still living with the same three girls and the party scene, but because I saw firsthand the possibilities of secure family life through my new influential people, I was ready to work hard for something more. I knew exactly what I wanted, and I desperately sought after it. I wanted a baby. So did Andy.

We knew what we were doing wasn't smart in any way. We were in the exact situation we had been in just six months prior, but this felt so different to me. I was mentally ready. I saw the possibilities of what life could be like if I walked a different path than those around me. I needed redemption for the choice I had made. I was changed, and I knew deep inside I would never forgive myself or never fully be happy unless I was a mom. I had a month-long break from school, so I went home to spend time with my family and Andy. I drove the three hours to my hometown with a hole in my heart, longing for it to be filled. A month later, when I drove back to my college town, I drove back feeling complete. It was like the hole in my heart was healed and my whole life was going to change for the better.

I knew I was pregnant the second it happened, but I obviously had to wait a few weeks for a pregnancy test to confirm it. When I saw those two lines, I broke down the same way I broke down the first time. This time, though, they were happy tears. In my heart, I thought I would be punished and never be redeemed for what I had done. But here I was—God was giving me another chance to be a mom, and I would never take that for granted.

When I told people I was pregnant, just like the last time, most of them weren't overly excited for us. I wasn't asking anyone for approval or advice, so no one was trying to talk us out of it, but no one was jumping for joy either. We were twenty-one and were living three hours apart. I was in the middle of my first of four years in a grueling doctorate program and was working very minimal hours as an intern for my schooling. Nothing in our situation was ideal. But we did not care. We were so in love with the baby boy growing within me we couldn't see anything else.

Andy packed up his things and moved to my town within a month of finding out I was pregnant-something he didn't even mention the first time. He found a job that gave him the flexibility to be home with the baby while I was at school. We were living the dream. We had barely any money and relied on his parents and my grandma to help us often, but we felt okay because we were finally different. We were finally going to authentically be ourselves, even if it looked different from everyone around us. We were finally becoming a family.

Months prior, I was begging God, through my regretful cries, to give me another chance. I knew, if God would entrust me with another life, I would be the best mother and raise this baby to know what a mighty, forgiving, and abundant God we have. In my heart, though, I didn't think He would. I thought I would be punished for the rest of my life for this. However, that isn't how God works. It is written in Psalms that "[God] has not punished us as we deserve for all our sins, for His mercy toward those who fear and honor him is as great as the height of the heavens above earth." (Psalm 103:10-11, TLB). I didn't understand that kind of mercy then.

As the weeks passed and my belly grew, I felt more forgiven though never fully. However, the moment our son, Noah, came into the world, I knew exactly what God meant when it was written His mercy extends to the heights of the heavens above Earth. He was healthy, beautiful, and everything I ever wanted. The love I felt toward my son and from God extended far beyond Earth into Heaven. Noah is living proof

God is a forgiving and loving God, able to redeem any choice, regret, or mistake you may make. There hasn't been a day since his birth, ten years ago, I haven't looked at him and thanked God for him.

For the next few years, Andy and I were so consumed with our little family, I barely remember anything else that happened surrounding us. I don't remember what my mom was doing or my family or close friends, and I barely even remember school, even though that consumed almost as much time as a newborn. I was so enamored with our new life, I refused to let anything else in that could distract me from it. We lived for a year and a half in my college town, until we couldn't take it any longer and packed up to move back home. Having a family as a college student, living in a college town was isolating.

Even though I still had friends, we had less in common, and it was hard to relate and communicate with each other. I must admit though, I did get bitter, mostly when it came to my best friend from high school (my previous roommate). We had been through everything together. We had been best friends since middle school, basically holding each other's hand through every stage of life so far, during some pretty tough times. When I got pregnant, and my entire life shifted, in some sense, I was also expecting hers to do the same. I wanted her to walk through this part of life with me, but she couldn't. She continued on her own path; her focus never shifted.

Looking back on it now with ten more years of wisdom, I understand. It would have been impossible for her to grasp how motherhood changes a person until she walked through it herself. I was expecting something from her she literally could not give to me. I was also doing the same to her, even though I didn't see it. My focus was entirely on my family, and it felt equally impossible for me to show awareness of the things taking place in her life. Our friendship suffered greatly. There was still love and friendship between us, but it took a long time to move past our hurt.

Moving back home to our family and a place where I knew a few people who were walking down our same path seemed to be the best option for us. We felt like we had so much support. We got married at this beautiful beach church surrounded by all our friends and family from home and college town. It was a beautiful, transitional beginning to our new life at home. Life felt good. We were finally living out this amazing dream that had been kept in our hearts for so long, and I didn't have to be ashamed about it here!

Surrounding myself with family and other friends in our exact same situation helped me grow as a mother and a wife. My circle of friends was small, but we were able to walk with each other in such a critical time of growth and transition. They walked beside me through toddler tantrums or our first argument as a married couple. I needed that tremendously, and I was so thankful for them. I realized through my journey into motherhood how important relationships were. I honestly thought the concept of friendship was created so you could have a few people to have a good time and laugh with. But it is so much more than that.

Having the right people beside you as you walk through critical periods of your life can completely change your perspective, and it can change the outcome of how you respond to your life. I knew I had to devote my attention to my family, and the only way I was able to do that was to surround myself with people who were doing the same. I wouldn't have become the mom or the wife I am without the environment I chose to immerse myself in.

Why Does This Even Matter?

What I have loved most about book writing is reliving experiences that were really frustrating or painful and seeing how that piece of my story was the most transformative aspect of it all. I have rarely walked through a painful experience and said to myself, "I bet God is about to create something beautiful out of this." Instead, I often question God and his reasonings for whatever I felt such as pain, loneliness, abandonment, anger, etc. For the past few months, while writing this book, I have had to put myself back into the emotions of my past. It has been tough at times because I can feel the hurt and regret all over again. This chapter has been a special chapter to write, however, and one that has given me a new appreciation of how intricately and intentionally God prepares your path. So many beautiful friendships and a lot of wisdom came from this really challenging time in my life. Without writing this book, I don't know if I would have even realized all of that frustration and hurt ended up being the greatest gift.

We have all heard something similar to, "You are the average of the five people you spend the most time with." It took me some time before I really understood what that meant. For starters, I have four children and a husband. If that quote truly applied to me, I would be completely dependent, demanding, cry at the drop of a hat, or be a man. It took some research to understand what "people" this was referring to and how to apply it to my life. Before we dive into how to come up with the best five people for your life, I want to go over the three types of relationships that are most prevalent in your life at any given moment. All relationships serve a purpose and are necessities to living a fulfilled life. It just takes the understanding of expectations and boundaries with each type of relationship to be able to construct a happy, goal-oriented environment for your life.

The first type of relationship is family. Overcoming expectations is one of the hardest, yet most freeing things you can do when it comes to family. I have read from different sources on the issue of toxicity in families that, in summary, it is okay to cut toxic family members out of your life. I believe this connects to the "you are the five people you surround yourself with" principle. No one wants to be surrounded with toxicity, and if we only have five people to choose as our surroundings, then I surely don't want it to be a negative person!

I feel like God uniquely designed families separate from friendships for a purpose. When we shift our expectations of family versus friends, I believe we will find some peace and acceptance when it comes to family. When I had my son, the first thing people mentioned in regards to our relationship was unconditional love. And yes, that is exactly what I felt the moment I looked over and he opened his little eyes to me. I knew from that point forward, no matter what he did in his life, I would love him. I have the same love for my mom (and my cousins, aunt, nieces, nephews, in-laws, etc). I love them. I cherish them. I believe our family was uniquely chosen for us. Because of that, I love them at their best and at their worst. However, love has boundaries.

We have to be careful our love for family doesn't cross the boundary to enable destructive behavior. The Bible gives us direct guidelines when it comes to handling any relationship that causes division: "If people are causing divisions among you, give a first and second warning. After that, have nothing more to do with them" (Titus 3:10-11, NLT). Love for the family may be unconditional, but loving can take place without allowing others' negativity to penetrate into your own heart and life. I could honestly write an entire book on this subject. For now, though, I want you to know setting high expectations for people that are given to us (family) almost always leads to disappointment. Love your family for who they are even if you don't always agree, just like you need the same love at times. While we may love them, we must create strict boundaries if their values, lifestyle, or negativity is great enough to penetrate into your own life.

The second type of friendship is the friend who you love so deeply you would consider them family. These are your lifelong friends. I probably have ten lifelong friends. In the age of social media, it is easy to stay in touch with people fairly regularly. I started loving these people at a very young age and never stopped. I view this group of friends just slightly higher on the totem pole than family when it comes to expectations. These relationships you get to choose, and they shouldn't be forced, so there is a standard of honesty, loyalty, and trust that definitely comes with them. It is nearly impossible to stay completely connected with a friend throughout your entire life. Circumstances change, people change, locations change, and people get disconnected. I have dear lifelong friends who are on a very different path than I am on, and some of us have very different values. Our friendship stays real because we understand we can love each other and be honest with one another, without being in constant communication.

The third type of relationship (the first is family and the second is lifelong friends) is almost the opposite of what I just described for the first two. This type of friend is a seasonal friend. Ten years ago, my jaw would have hit the floor if I had seen myself writing this now. I just didn't believe in something called a seasonal friend. In my eyes, at the time, that sounded like a fake friendship. It felt like if a friendship only lasted a season, that meant someone would be left feeling hurt and used in the end. In the past five years, I have come to understand and appreciate the value of seasonal friendships, and I want you to understand them too. Have you ever heard of a group called MOPS? It's a group for moms of preschool students. It was created for moms to find community and friendships with other moms who were in the same stage of life. Of course, women find lifetime friends from that group. But most importantly, they find friends to walk through that season of life with. It is such a special and fundamental type of friendship. This is the type of friendship that is crucial when it comes to choosing your environment.

I didn't realize it at the time, but that is what I was desperately searching for when I moved back to my hometown. I needed to be the best mom and wife I could possibly be, but I had zero examples around me. When I moved home and surrounded myself with family members who were amazing examples of healthy marriages and friends who adored their children, I started to evolve into that. That wasn't my expectation, but when it happened, I came to understand what it meant to be the average of the five people you surround yourself with.

Over the next five years, as our life changed as life does, I noticed those friendships I desperately needed as a new mom began to fade. That's when I began to understand what seasonal friendship was. There had been no arguments or hard feelings, but our lives started shifting and didn't align as they once did. Seasonal friendships serve such a specific and significant purpose in our life. We need companionship to guide us through shifting seasons in our lives, and these unique and beautiful friendships give us that.

I have also realized in time, some friends stick by our

sides forever. One of my best friends and I have seemed to go down the same life path since day one. We have never had an off-season, and our friendship continually grows. There were other friendships that seemed to be seasonal but developed into lifelong friendships. I thought my best friend from high school/college roommate was a seasonal friend for a while. We had been through hardships together, had fun together, and encouraged each other to do well in sports and school. However, our friendship faded fast when I was pregnant and became a new mom and she was still living college life.

Although it was hard, I had accepted that maybe our friendship hadn't stood the test of time. However, over the course of a few years, she got married and started a family of her own. It was incredible to watch our friendship evolve from the rocky place it had been to something new. My love for her has exponentially grown from the time we were college students. Right now, she is a role model when it comes to health, mothering, and marriage. Our seasonal friendship has become a lifelong friendship and one I am proud to have among the "five people closest" to me.

I feel like I went over a lot when it comes to defining certain friendships. I do hope you have a clearer picture of the types of friendships and how they play certain roles in your life. But honestly, this chapter isn't really about friendships. It is about you and how you are going to grow into the best person you can be.

Here is your life application for this chapter:

Step 1: Look at the relationships in your life and see what kind of unrealistic expectations you have for these people. Group your people into categories of Family, Lifelong Friends, and Seasonal Friends. Once your people are in groups, write, in bold print, at the top of the list, your expectation for them. We all have our own expectations for the relationships in our lives. My expectation for family is unconditional love and having boundaries. Maybe your family dynamic is very toxic, so creating and maintaining boundaries plays a crucial role in your expectations. However, some families are very close to one another, so love and friendship intermingle, and creating boundaries may be less important. My expectations for lifelong friendships include trust and honesty. For seasonal friendships, I expect to grow from them. These expectations aren't necessarily for the people in your life but for you and how you view that relationship. It is a constant evaluation of how intentional you are with your relationships and how you let those around you dictate your future.

Step 2: Go back to the work we did in the last chapter, look at the goals listed, and find people who are an example of those goals. I'll use my own as an example. I want to be a marathon runner, fully devoted to living out God's purpose for my life, an intentional mom and wife, and an author. Those are long-term goals, and they can seem impossible if I dwell in that place. However, instead of being paralyzed by lofty goals and not knowing how to achieve them, focus on people that are farther along on the same journey. I can make a list of people who are examples of each of these things—a runner, a writer, a leader at my church, a mom, and a wife I admire. These people need to be part of your five with whom you surround yourself!

I am not talking about the people who are the very best at these, although that would be ideal. But at the very least, choose someone who is also striving to be better in the same areas you are striving to be better in. As a Christ-believer, that is why I find a church to be so important. You are surrounded by like-minded people that both encourage you and hold you accountable to live out a godly lifestyle. Find a way to create your list of people who inspire you to live out your dreams simply by watching them live out theirs.

To go further with this, follow every single person you can on social media who have "made it" in the category in which you want to succeed. Watch what you consume. If you have a goal to have a healthy lifestyle but follow food blogs and pages where people consume alcohol regularly, you may not realize how much that can steer you off course. Social media has a sneaky way of influencing your decisions through other people's pictures and lifestyles. Unfollow the accounts that deter you from your dream life.

Believe it or not, there isn't a magical method to becoming the average of the five people you surround yourself with. It is just how it works. If you constantly surround yourself with negativity and hate, you will, no matter how hard you try not to, start to be filled with negativity and hate yourself. Beth Moore explained she can not go longer than a day without reading her Bible because, if she does, it allows other things to trickle into her mind and get her off track of being completely devoted to Jesus.[3] Be like Beth! Be completely devoted to being your greatest self, and don't let anything stand in your way.

As a child, a famous football star lived in the same neighborhood as another famous football star. He was able to normalize becoming a professional football player because he saw it firsthand everyday. It became more than a dream to him...it became real to him! His dream became something not just reserved for special people, but for everyday, normal people who worked hard for it. What you surround yourself with is what you become. Set your intentions and goals high. There is nothing wrong with having a standard of greatness for your life and who you surround yourself with.

Every relationship I have had in my life is sacred to me. I have never intentionally ended a friendship because if there is love in me, it stays for life. You can love someone and check in on them without indulging in their lifestyle. I left where I lived, not to end friendships, but to become the best mom I could be. I am doing the same thing today—constantly shifting who I allow in my circle to make room to become a better version of myself. If you do this work, I promise you, in a short matter of time, you will find yourself excited about all of the possibilities for your future. You can become who you want to be. You just have to have the best tools (people) surrounding you.

Six
PREPARE YOURSELF FOR BATTLE

The next few years went by like a dream. My life was coming together, piece by piece, into something more beautiful than I ever could have imagined. It started with my engagement, as troubled as I was at the time. But once I started really living out my life, on my terms, instead of everyone else's, I felt true happiness. When Noah came into our lives, the blessings were overflowing. Being a mother changed me. I was so conscious of God's forgiveness to me, and I wanted to honor Him with how I took on this new role of being a wife and a mother. I knew being a wife and a mother was such a precious gift, and because of this, I was determined to soak it up and do it right. Andy went back to the job that was waiting for him, and I finished up my last few years of pharmacy school.

You know how people say you wait your whole life to be an adult, and then when it comes, it totally sucks? I can relate to that *now* when I am doing endless amounts of laundry… but then? I love being an adult. On my twenty-fifth birthday, I remember lying on the couch while it was raining outside. I was starting to drift off for a midday nap, listening to the rain trickle on our roof, tired, because I was newly pregnant with our second child, our first daughter. I looked over at Andy and said, "This is what I have waited my whole life for." I didn't want any gifts, a birthday party, or anything at all. When I looked at what I had, I knew I already had it all.

Exactly two years later, on my twenty-seventh birthday, I was in the exact same spot looking around. Except for this time, our house was a little louder with two kids running around, and I was pregnant with our third child and our second baby girl. Again, I looked at Andy and asked, "How can this be our life?" Surely, it doesn't get better. Our life had definitely gotten harder, but it was *good*. It was filled with love. Every time I was pregnant, someone would always tell me to hold on to these moments because these years fly by. Even if they said it as one of my kids was having a tantrum in aisle three of the grocery store, I never got annoyed. I knew they were speaking from experience, so I really tried to hold on to every single moment, even the hard ones.

As my babies would lie asleep beside me, I would stare at them, trying to memorize every feature on their tiny little faces. In the afternoon, as we were all playing outside, I would take a step back and just watch. Their songs of "Ring around the Rosie" and roars of laughter would fill my ears, and I would try to tuck them away in my heart, just praying those sounds would ring just as loudly, even when I am eighty years old. As I soaked up those moments, trying to burn those perfect memories into my mind, sometimes a thought would creep in that I tried to quickly push out. Even as fleeting as the thought was, I knew there was truth to it.

"You know this isn't forever; right? You know there will be pain. You know there will be hurt. Brace yourself. One day it will come."

As much as I wanted to tell myself the thought was the devil in my mind, I truly don't think it was. I wish I could say he was trying to take over my thoughts and make me unappreciative of the moment I was living in. This is life, though, and we must know that even if we have gotten to the top of our mountain where we have reached our goal, happy ending, or our dream life, *storms can still come*. There can be a rain shower; a temporary hard time in the midst of an otherwise optimal chapter of your life. Or there could be a raging storm that comes through and rips up the life and happiness you have been living. Life can feel perfect, but heartache can hit in an instant out of nowhere. I don't say this for you to live in negativity and have a looming fear that tragedy will strike any minute. Enjoy your beautiful life, and soak up all of the wonderful moments. That is what life is about. I just want, in some way, to equip you with the knowledge of how to walk through the storms (if they ever come) with strength and power. If you know how to prepare, you can walk into worrying times braver. That is exactly what I did on October 15th, 2015.

Andy and I had the day off together because it was a day we had been looking forward to for weeks. It was our doctor's appointment to confirm the pregnancy of our third child. It had come as a shock to us that we had gotten pregnant so quickly after our second baby was born, but we were thrilled to have a growing family. As we sat in the waiting room, I let my nervous jitters take over, and I began bouncing my legs up and down waiting for my name to be called. I was nervous that day for two reasons. First, the sound of that first heartbeat and the confirmation that there is a baby growing inside of me is always a very special day to me. Secondly, I was anxious, waiting for a phone call.

My grandma also had a doctor's appointment that day to get a cyst checked out. My aunt went with her and promised to call as soon as the appointment was finished. Still sitting in the waiting room, my phone rang. I looked down to see it was my aunt, so I stepped outside quickly to answer it. I was expecting the usual clean bill of health for my grandma and for my aunt to tell me they were on the way home. Instead, on the other end, my aunt sounded panicked and worried. She told me they were still at the doctor's office and it wasn't a good visit. The doctor suspected something was very wrong with my grandma and needed to run some tests. Before they took my grandma back to run the tests, they bluntly told each of them to prepare for the worst. That was all she knew at the moment, but she told me to do the same: **prepare for the worst.** I could barely finish the call before my name was called for my doctor's visit. I quickly told her I loved her and I would be waiting for her next call with more news.

Before the doctor came into the room, I let the reality of what my aunt had said sink in. I was replaying the past week in my head and beating myself up for not catching on to the signs that my grandma knew something that we didn't. I *knew* something seemed wrong when she told us about the appointment, but I didn't want to believe it when I heard trembling in her voice as she told us about the "cysts." I had a sinking feeling my aunt would call me back with terrible news. Because of those thoughts, I let my head fall into my hands and quietly cried. I was not expecting the day to go like this. I was not expecting to feel heartache on a day that was supposed to bring so much joy to my husband and me. When the doctor walked in, I could barely dry my tears before she placed the doppler over my stomach.

Lub-dub, lub-dub, lub-dub.

There it was. My first time hearing the heartbeat of my baby girl, growing and healthy in my belly. Tears once again streamed down my face, and I thought to myself, *How strange is this feeling?* I am crying both tears of sadness and tears of joy at the same time. Until that moment, I didn't know those two feelings could co-exist on the same day, let alone in the exact same moment. I was suddenly looking at life through a completely new lens. The reality that bad and good, heartache and joy, or death and life could co-exist together felt strangely liberating to me but also very terrifying. I had always thought it was one or the other. You could only be happy or sad. That is why I was so afraid of that voice in my head. I thought that when the sadness came, I wouldn't have any of the good parts of my life anymore. It was freeing to know that whatever news I might receive, I would still be able to hold tight to the happiness I had in my growing family and the love I had for my grandmother. But it was also terrifying to imagine the depth of the pain I might feel when I finally got the news.

A few hours later, I sat outside enjoying the breezy fall weather with my daughter, as I was waiting for the follow-up call. The phone finally rang, and my stomach sank when I saw that it was my aunt again. I looked at my phone and whispered to myself, "Brace yourself, Riki-Leigh." I immediately could hear the frightened tone in my aunt's voice as I said *hello*. She could barely speak and was holding back tears. Despite the broken sentences, I was able to piece together what she was trying to tell me. She didn't want to be there alone. Why didn't anyone go with her to take my grandma to this appointment? Stage four cancer. Two months to live.

Two months to live.

How can anyone even brace themselves for that type of impact? Because of the first call, I was expecting bad news. I was expecting cancer. I had already been bracing myself for what I thought was the worst-case scenario, but I was thinking treatments, nausea, and hair falling out. Absolute worst-case scenario, I was expecting years. Two *months* never crossed my mind. My heart was instantly shattered. The phone call was short, and once she hung up, the world somehow looked completely different than it did just two minutes prior. I looked around to find Andy, and my legs felt weak. I wish I could tell you I sobbed, felt like I couldn't breathe, or fell to the ground and begged for it not to be true. But instead, I just looked at him and said, "This is it." He was puzzled, but it didn't matter. I knew what I meant. That fleeting thought I had been pushing from my mind so many times had come back. This time it said, "This is it. This is what you have been preparing for."

In moments like these, there isn't much time to sit around and arrange an elaborate plan. It wasn't a question of *if* my heart would be broken or *if* I was going to allow this to hurt me—that was a done deal. There are moments in life when you don't get the choice to be hurt or not. You *will* hurt and your heart *will* be shattered, no matter what steps you have taken to prevent it. The question then becomes, how will you navigate through the pain? How will you walk through this unplanned and unwanted journey of pain with intention? How do you grow and learn from this and let it shape you into someone stronger? How do you not let it break you down into something you didn't want to become?

By the time I got off the phone with my aunt on that day, I was in preparation. That day, I made a hard, yet necessary decision to metaphorically put on battle gear every single day of her sickness. Normally, if there was a stressful situation in our family, my grandma would handle it. She was the mediator. Metaphorically putting on battle gear, to me, was taking on the role of my grandma. It meant to constantly reduce tensions, listen to everyone's problems, resolve conflicts, without getting the others involved, and the hardest of all, to not take anything personally while doing it.

I knew my grandma's sickness and ultimate death would cause so much stress, fear, and worry, that managing tensions would be inevitable. Because I intimately knew my family, I knew how they would react. We all put some type of guard up, but we all do it differently. I knew that one person's grief would turn into anger. I knew that another person's grief would be a roller coaster, completely unpredictable and unreliable. I knew that one would grieve in silence and distance themselves. I knew that my own grief would push those closest to me away, in a futile attempt to protect myself. My grandma knew this. She knew how to handle all of us. But this time, I could not let her do that. My defense mechanism became taking every emotional hit there was for the sake of letting my grandma die in peace. I made a commitment to myself that my grandma would come first, and I would come last, no matter how much it hurt.

Although our family is large, including distant cousins and kids, the family that was going to be directly impacted by my grandma's cancer was pretty small: myself, my mom, my aunt, and one of my cousins. There were so many other people who cared, were hurt, and helped, but it would ultimately be up to the four of us to do the hard work. I didn't know this before her diagnosis, but there is so much responsibility that falls on caretakers when it comes to cancer or any illness, I suppose. It seemed overwhelming to take it all in, understand the treatment plan, and then move into action simultaneously. I knew we could do the hard work for my grandma, but I also knew how we all processed stress and heartache. I had witnessed it my entire life during different situations of conflict. We could check the boxes and do what was needed, but when it came to processing loss and letting ourselves actually feel the pain, we put our guards up.

I had never observed anyone from my family cry at a funeral or during a stressful situation. I understood it then, and I understand it now because I am the same way. It is so much easier on the heart to have a job or help in some way during tragedy because sitting in the pain and feeling it can sweep you off your feet and consume you. Everyone took their own excruciating turn doing the hard work, whether it was sitting at the doctor's office with her or going with her to pick out her casket. No one got out of this without their own unique wound. It was an agonizing journey for all of us, but we did what was needed.

I wasn't prepared to lose her, and I wasn't prepared for the total chaos that surrounded her sickness, but I was ready to take this heartbreaking journey by her side. The voice in my head had been telling me all along, *soak it up while you have it*. And I did. We all did. We sat down with her, watched her, and listened to her stories. We rocked with her on the front porch and held her hand when she got sick from the chemo. The early days of her diagnosis were bittersweet but more on the sweet side. Our family came together and showered her with love. We took her on a girls' trip to New York City, we had a huge Thanksgiving celebration, full of family and friends, and we sat together laughing and reminiscing about good times.

I never let her see my pain or suffering because I wanted her to feel at peace with having to leave us. As cancer progressed, however, so did the tensions in my family. It was one blow after the next, consistent and fierce because the pain everyone was processing and feeling had grown exponentially. I never blamed anyone because I had signed up for this, but that didn't make it easier. As the end was getting closer, the harder it became for all of us to keep it together. There were arguments over everything, from how often she got sick, to how another person grieved, to who came and visited more. One person would spiral with anger, while the other would spiral with alcohol.

I don't want to say I handled everything perfectly because I know I didn't. However, because I was pregnant, I was very intentional about how I was going to take care of my body and mind during this time. I think pregnancy was a gift to me during this time and the reason I felt so prepared to take on this emotional battle. There were so many behind-the-scenes fires that I desperately put out before my grandma could see them. She often looked at me, barely able to keep her eyes open, and asked me with a weak voice, "What's happening that you don't want me to see?" But each time, I just kissed her head and told her everything was fine; we just loved her. That was the truth. She was so loved, and we were so heartbroken.

We got her two months longer than the doctors expected, but it could never have been long enough for our hearts. It was grueling to be there for the end of her life. Nothing quite prepares you for the way that cancer comes in and rips apart someone's body, their life, and their family in just a short four-month span. But it did, and we were forced to cope.

On the day she died, after I said my final goodbye to her, I returned home to finally get some rest. My husband took the kids out for the day so I could rest my seven-month pregnant body and sleep away the day's heartbreak. I distinctly remember feeling a wave of relief wash over me. Is that wrong to say? I don't know if you have ever walked through an expected death like this, but the day of death didn't seem to be as hard as everything else had been. I had a ton of grief to process, but on that day, my body felt relief. I wasn't glad this journey was over. I wanted her back with me, sick or not. But I was both physically and mentally tired. Being the punching bag for everyone's grief was something I was ready for, but I never knew how brutal it was going to be for me. There were times when I wanted to break down and beg God to make it all stop, but I always came back to that voice in my head. I knew I was made for times like this. I believed because of our hard work, she had died in peace. I was finally able to take the weight of that gear off. Everyone would have to grieve on their own, disagree on their own, express frustrations on their own. I was done.

For months, I had diffused arguments and helped people get themselves together, but now I had no tolerance for it. It was my turn to shut the world out and live my life the way I wanted. I used the two months I had left of my pregnancy to turn my phone off and soak up my family. I didn't use my time to grieve. Instead, I found happiness I had not experienced for months. I missed a big piece of my heart, but I let her love live through me. I loved my kids the exact way she loved me.

When Eden Grace (a name my grandma had helped me choose) was born, I was so ready for a fresh start in life. I called Eden my calm after the storm. I felt like I had been living in a storm for six months: hurting, grieving, and fighting to stay brave, and I felt like this was the end. I decided to have a natural labor with her, and as I was in labor, in the middle of the most agonizing pain, I kept telling myself to push through (literally) until the end. The end of the pain and my reward was the baby girl I would soon meet. When I looked into Eden's eyes, I felt like she was hand-picked from my grandma and given straight to me. Having her in my arms gave me hope for a better future. I was ready to pick back up where I'd left off, with the life I had right before any of this mess, the life I loved, that was filled with happiness.

Why Does This Even Matter?

We live on the coast, so at least once a year we have to prepare for hurricane season. In good years, all we have to do is just acknowledge it is hurricane season and watch the weather channel relatively often. But other years, we actually get a hurricane. I dread the day the meteorologist says to get prepared because I know we have days of work ahead of us. We need to get gas for our generator, board up the windows, bring in our outdoor toys, and load up on non-perishable food. After that is complete, we sit inside and wait for the storm to come.

What would happen if we didn't prepare for the hurricane? Honestly, some years nothing would happen. Sometimes the hurricane just feels like a little thunderstorm. The other years? If we did not prepare, the effects of the storm would be devastating. We wouldn't survive the damage. That is how I went into my grandma's sickness. I knew if I went into this journey without preparing myself, I wouldn't survive. How do we go into painful and devastating times in a way that prepares us like we would for hurricane season?

Here is your life application for this chapter:

Step 1: Know that life could end at any moment.

When I first had my son, I was consumed with the thought of death. I was terrified I would die, and he would be left motherless. As I got carried away with the thought of death, I started to be afraid he would die. This consumed me, and I imagined him one day being consumed with the thought of death as well. I don't know what compelled me to do this, but I Googled the age children understand death. There are a few steps children go through to understand it, but almost all children fully understand death by seven years old. He would still be fragile and innocent at seven. I could go on about the spiral I went on about him having to grasp that concept, but the point of it all is what I started to ask myself. If almost every person knows by seven years old that death is irreversible and universal, then why aren't we acting like it? Why are we still walking around arguing about who took the trash out instead of thanking our husband for the coffee waiting for us? Why are we pushing our kids out of the car at drop-off instead of looking them in the eye and telling them we love them as they start their day?

This might sound ludicrous, but when those thoughts come into my head, I am not thinking about how damaging it is to the other person. I *know* it is, and I feel like we should always be pouring out our love to others. I know if my husband dies tomorrow, he will be in perfect peace in Heaven. He won't be thinking about my last dramatic sigh to him about the trash not being taken out. Do you know who will be thinking about that though, wishing to do it over again? Me. Or you, if a loved one passes away.

Live a life in which you don't have to wonder what you said last to a person. Know it was filled with love. I know we all mess up, and I personally mess up every single day. Yet, if we acknowledge that any moment could be not *our last*, but *their last*, wouldn't that change how we love? Let that be how you go through your day and go through the rest of your life.

Step 2: Imagine who you want to be at the end of this.

Have you ever been through a trauma or a tragedy? Can you relate when I say it feels similar to a gut punch? When tragedy strikes, it knocks the wind out of us. Certain tragedies deliver such a blow, we can't even imagine how life could possibly go on. I understand that. Even though I think this tool is one of the most important in preparing yourself in a time of tragedy, I also know this may be hard to do in some situations. When I got the call that my grandma had two months to live, it immediately changed my life. I feel grateful I was pregnant at the time because instead of reaching for a drink to numb out the pain, I had to find another way to cope. That's when I discovered this major tool in my life.

After that phone call, I took a few minutes and envisioned what life could possibly look like in a few months. I realized everyone's life was about to completely fall apart, and the only thing I would have control over was how I reacted and who I would become from this journey. As I sat and "put on my battle gear," I listed out my priorities. My battle gear was my mindset walking into this experience.s. I laid out my intentions for this journey, and even though it hurt, I allowed those intentions to steer me through the unknown.

Priority number one: give my grandma peace. I knew this one was going to be hard because I would have to diffuse problems before they ever reached her. I had never done this before because she was the mediator of the family. It was important to me that I achieved this because I didn't want her to feel like she had unfinished business when she left us. My second priority was to come out stronger. I wanted to be intentional in how I dealt with everything we would go through. I began reading through the book of Job in the Bible right as my grandma received her diagnosis. I was amazed at the parallels between his trials and my own.

In just the first few chapters, Job lost all of his livestock, his servants, and, most heart-wrenching to me, he lost his children. Despite his extreme loss, he declared, "...The Lord gave, and the Lord has taken away; Blessed be the name of the Lord" (Job 1:21, NKJV). I wanted to be like Job. I wanted to still believe God was good. I wanted my faith to be unwavering, and I wanted everyone around me to see that. I knew this would be the first example my children would experience of losing someone, and I knew they would be relying on me to walk with them through it. I cried when I needed to cry. I sat and enjoyed the moments with my grandmother whenever I could. I tried to create lasting memories we all could share together. Staying intentional about my priorities was exhausting, but it was necessary. Without setting that intention at the beginning, I would have fallen apart, and my family would have fallen apart with me. Having sight of the bigger picture is key to walking through tragedy and coming out of it stronger.

I know there are tragedies that will hit you like you never expected. They could bring heartache, loss, and even death. When we experience a huge tragedy, we often aren't equipped to immediately find some type of silver lining in those tragedies. We can't immediately set out intentions and plans when grief hits us. We can't see what good could possibly come from it, no matter how hard we try. I am not giving you the impractical advice to go skipping through tragedy because of some "bigger purpose" awaiting on the other side. I am asking from you, friend, the exact same thing I asked from myself many years ago. *Plan now for future heartache*. Layout your intentions *now* for grief that may (hopefully) never happen.

If you have tucked in the back of your mind that you need to be prepared for pain, however small or big it may be, then when tragedy happens, you can stop and remember that envisioned image of yourself emerging on the other side of hurt, whenever that may be. When you see your future self, are you stronger? Are you wiser? Are you more patient? Are you an advocate or an activist for a cause that once caused you heartache? Do you walk through life more slowly, soaking up all of the beautiful pieces that surround you? Whatever your intention is, it is right for you. It doesn't have to be elaborate. My intention was to simply let my grandma die in peace and to come out stronger. That was my battle gear. To come out stronger will be my battle gear if I ever have to face something similar. I have my intentions in my mind now. I wake up every day with that stronger self on my mind. Set the intention right away so you know that even though you hurt, you grieve, and maybe you are angry, you will still get through it with some part of who you are left.

I have a friend whose close relative was a drug addict for as long as I can remember. She was incredibly sweet and hilarious, but she struggled a lot. Last week, that relative died. When I talk to my friend about them, she is a complete mess. It is heartbreaking to see and hear. But to me, it is even more heartbreaking to watch my friend slip. Normally fierce and independent, she has begun drinking and taking pills to cope. I want to shake her and tell her to stop so she doesn't recreate for her kids the same life she had growing up. However, I feel like if someone is already in the midst of grieving, having set no intentions for their future self, then it is difficult to stop in the middle, create some intention, and continue to grieve. That is why I think it is so important to tell you this before you ever have to deal with something so big. You will get through it. You just have to be prepared to come out of it stronger than you were before you entered it.

Step 3: Remember Yourself in the Midst of the War.

I have always known that I tend to put others' needs before my own. I used to consider it a badge of honor. Now, however, I can see the consequences of putting yourself last. I am an Enneagram type two. An Enneagram two is called The Helper. I have taken the test so many times and even swapped out the answers and STILL get a two. I don't understand, except that I must be so much of a two that it even picks up when I am lying. I know all of the great qualities about being a two like always volunteering, participating in service projects, and making people feel loved and good about themselves. But it feels like a punch in the gut each time I see my results because I know the ramifications.

When my grandma was sick, my willingness to be the helper and nurturer was both a blessing and a curse. The problem was I was always the last person allowed to grieve. My main goal was to keep my grandma at peace. But I let it go farther than that. Instead of just putting out fires so my grandma didn't have to see any behind-the-scenes drama, I let myself take on the grief of other people. It was mentally taxing. While it was happening, I justified it because of my grandma. But the longer it happened, I realized it wasn't serving me at all. Instead, it was greatly damaging me. When it was all over, I felt like I had completely lost myself.

Can you relate to that? As women (or a man), we are typically caregivers in some way. We provide a mother's touch, we are a daughter to elderly parents, and we are a shoulder to cry on for friends. Being a caregiver is such a beautiful title to hold. It is needed in this world. But how much is too much? Are you giving so much that you are losing yourself along the way? Is everyone around you able to find rest and comfort, but you realize that you aren't at all?

PREPARE YOURSELF FOR BATTLE

You have to remember that you are important too. You can be the caregiver and still care about yourself. Being the helper doesn't mean you are a walking mat for other people's grief. Believe it or not, you can only come out better if you make yourself a priority. You can be a helper and also help yourself. It is okay. You don't need permission to love yourself as much as the next person. Treat yourself like the gold you are. I like to imagine myself as my own kids. Would I let someone talk to them negatively or use them as a punching bag for grief? No way! If that answer is no for someone else, then it is no for you as well. You are your greatest possession. Take care of that person. You have to make it out of this battle too.

Seven

OWN UP

Just a few weeks after my daughter was born, I realized even though she gave me a new sense of hope and happiness, there was still pain. Three kids were a much harder adjustment than I had anticipated. The adjustment didn't come with the natural ease my first and second did, and I was really struggling. On top of that, I was still majorly dealing with the aftereffects of my grandma's death. I was overwhelmed with things I never anticipated, selling her house, processing her will, taking care of bills and life insurance, and getting knocked to the ground with my own waves of grief.

Once my grandma died, I purposely distanced myself from my family so I could find happiness again without being stuck with their grief. Instead of happiness though, I hurt just as bad, and I was alone in my pain. I was completely caught off guard with all of this, and I was frustrated. I had always taken pride in my ability to roll with the punches. When I mentally put on my battle gear the day my grandma was diagnosed, I felt proud of myself. I thought I had an advantage over everyone else; I would be able to take the pain. Now, I felt blindsided with grief and couldn't fully understand it enough to set any intentions for myself. I thought the battle was over. I thought I had already done the work. Naively, I thought you only fought hard battles once, and then it was over. Despite all of my preparation, I had not realized I would still have more work to do. I heard a pastor once say it isn't the first storm that takes you down. It's the second storm you create that changes your life. I made it through the first devastating loss of my grandmother, but the second storm was one I had created myself through stress, grief, and loneliness. I thought I was finally deserving enough for a break, but it never came.

One afternoon, after the diaper changes, sibling arguments, and protested nap times had left me feeling spent, I sent Andy an SOS text. I was ready for a break whenever he could leave work. I don't know what I expected at the time. Maybe a hot bath or a walk around the block by myself. When he got home though, he surprised me with a little gift. He said it would wash away the troubles of the day. And oh, was he right. A bottle of wine. Not what I was looking for but it felt so much better.

We had always been social drinkers and related alcohol to fun nights out. I was excited to let my hair down for the night and drink some wine. The wine reminded me of a night of fun and no responsibility. That first sip was everything I needed. The way it hit the back of my throat and warmed my belly. As I took another sip, I felt the anxiety melt away. I thought to myself, *this is exactly what I needed*. So, I chugged that first glass and finally let a smile creep back on my face. I could relax. I could enjoy my family. That bottle of wine was the escape I had been desperately searching for.

From that day forward, whenever I had a hard day (which was pretty often between the grief and the kids), I sent the same SOS text and got the same result. Andy loved it. He liked drinking too. He needed the stress relief, the break, the warmth in his belly, and a smile on his face. Soon, I didn't even have to ask for it. Without realizing what was happening or how harmful it could be, sharing a bottle of wine together became a daily habit.

That is how it starts-with addictions of every shape and size. Most people do not realize that their innocent starting point could lead to a lifetime of destruction or their rock bottom. For us, it was a glass of wine at night to ease the stress of the day. Then, it was two glasses a night. That worked better for the stress and the grief. Before long, those two glasses didn't cut it. I didn't want to feel just a wave of relief washing over me; I wanted to feel nothing at all. Because alcohol is so normalized in our society, it is hard to see alcoholism when it is staring you in the face. Every morning when I woke up with a pounding headache and feeling fuzzy for the first hour, I wondered if what we were doing had gotten out of hand. But, when I looked around for answers, I didn't find anything telling me to stop. There were t-shirts at Target, breakfast menus featuring mimosas, bars at movie theaters. Even though the nagging in my heart told me one thing, the world around me told me something entirely different.

From the day I sent the first SOS text to now months later, I was waiting for the moment when things would finally get easier for me. The wine helped the nights, but the days were agonizing. The hangovers made my already short fuse shorter, and it made the grief stronger. It was hard to put a smile on my face. Whenever someone turned their eyes on me, I would fall apart in my grief. When it was too early to drink, I ate. I was sure that when a year had passed after my grandma's death and Eden's birth, I would somehow be back to normal again. I felt like a year was an acceptable time to still be grieving/ struggling as a new-again mom, but anything longer than a year would probably be a little excessive.

I thought I had control over my grief and my alcohol

consumption. But when the year mark was about to hit, and I looked at myself, I didn't even recognize who I had become. There was no magic cure waiting for me at the year mark, and I knew that. The only thing that had materialized in a year was an extra thirty pounds and a fiery alcohol problem. We tried a few times to eliminate alcohol to see if it was the problem, but just as for my mom when she battled addiction, every time we stopped, it was like adding gasoline before coming back and lighting the match. My pain didn't stop when I stopped drinking, so I started again, a little heavier each time.

We moved to liquor, with which we could drink less and feel less. We were battling hangovers almost daily, and the only cure to a hangover was to count down until it was an acceptable time to drink again. When Eden's birthday came, I was crushed by the reality I wasn't the mom, the wife, or the person I thought I was going to be. That girl who snuck out of the room to check on her mom's breathing growing up, the college student who got a doctorate's degree while being the best mom and wife possible, and the woman who held her grandma's hair back while she was sick and dying; she was gone. Somewhere in all of this, I'd finally hit my breaking point, and I'd lost myself.

No one would ever know by looking at me from the outside, but Eden's first birthday was more of a day of misery than it was a celebration for me. I was dreading the moment when everyone arrived, all of the people I dearly loved. It was exhausting to pretend I was happy, and I was terrified of anyone finding out how much of a mess I was. Before the party started, I made a drink to calm my nerves and help my smile seem a little more genuine. It worked. A little while later, before we sang happy birthday, Andy and I snuck away to take two more shots. He jokingly said it was a celebration. We made it through the year with everyone alive. I downed the shot and wondered silently to myself, *did we really make it out alive? Because this feels pretty dead to me.*

I thought I had battled some tough demons in my life, but nothing kept me down as long as this one did. As the year passed, and I watched each new month come and go, I felt my grief shift from the loss of my grandma to the loss of my life. Everything seemed to be falling apart now. Something we began to ease our stress was now the cause of all of it. Alcohol brought out Andy's insecure and angry side and my sad and despondent side. Our two glasses of wine nights, the nights we stayed up, talked, and giggled about the craziness of our days were long gone. Now it was bickering with each other and sitting on opposite sides of the room on our phones in different worlds. Each morning, a wave of hopelessness would overcome me. I didn't see a way this could get better without walking away from alcohol, and I wasn't willing to do that yet.

Mine and Andy's relationship became dull. We loved each other deeply and were committed to giving our children the best. We put on happy faces for our children and our family, but after everyone was gone or asleep, we realized we barely even spoke to each other. We were drifting apart at a rapid pace, but we didn't realize alcohol was the problem. In the mornings, we promised each other better lives and a better relationship because we had clarity when we were sober. But as soon as the hangover kicked in, all we gave and all we got were empty promises. Our relationship was becoming so empty and loveless, despite both of us wanting more from ourselves and each other. I desperately wanted to quit drinking but knew I couldn't do it alone. At that time, he didn't want to quit. I thought there was no way out from the downward slope we were in. I thought this would be our forever.

The cycle had been a long one, and even though I hated it, it had become my normal. The cycle went completely off track though one early winter morning when I felt a pain I had felt before. A few times actually. Even though I knew this familiar feeling, I did not want to believe it. If it was true, I would have to change the path I was on. I knew I needed to change, but I knew it would be excruciating and hard. I didn't want to go through it, so I avoided my thoughts for a few days. A couple of days later, when the nagging in my heart became too much to bear, I forced myself to the store. Once I got home, I sat on the cold bathroom floor alone, wishing for a response I knew I wasn't getting. Two minutes and one word later, my life was changing again. I was pregnant with baby number four.

This positive test was not like the past three joy-filled ones. When I looked down and saw the result of the test, I was instantly brought back to a nineteen-year-old version of myself, devastated at the blow of this type of news. How could I let this happen? I honestly didn't even know how it happened because Andy and I hardly spoke to each other. I immediately went in a spiral, thinking of all of the reasons why this couldn't be happening to us. Not now.

Our marriage.

We were barely hanging on by a thread. Three kids threw us for a loop we weren't prepared for. What would four kids do to us? Would we even make it to that point?

My kids.

My baby Eden didn't even get to be the family baby for long. She would hate us. Noah and Adella had been there through our year-long spiral. Our life would get so much worse now, and they would have to endure it all.

The baby.

No baby deserves parents who aren't excited. How could I let myself be unprepared again?

Myself.

Oh…me. I was falling apart. I was fragile. I was depressed. I had an alcohol problem. I knew what I desperately needed to do. I needed to spend time focusing on myself. I needed to get healthy and get my mind right. It seemed so simple but such a daunting task. I had no idea how to focus on myself to get healthy while focusing on a newborn baby. I envisioned my life spiraling out of control as soon as the baby was born, just like it had before. I felt so much shame for not being happy about this pregnancy. Even though I would now have the chance to break free from the alcohol, the shame of having another unplanned pregnancy drove my depression deeper.

The first few months were a fog of nausea, fatigue, and sadness. The only thing I was looking forward to was a trip to Mexico that was coming up right as I was hitting my four-month mark in pregnancy. We had planned this trip to Mexico before I had gotten pregnant, and even though I was initially envisioning cocktails on the beach, I was still really looking forward to this trip. A few weeks before we were set to leave, I decided to talk to my doctor about the funk I was still in. I still felt alone in a room full of people. I still cried, and I still felt shame about who I was. I thought the break from alcohol would have cured that, but I was still there. I needed help getting unstuck, and my doctor's visit was my first attempt. She prescribed me an antidepressant to start, along with a follow-up in a few weeks to monitor how I was feeling.

I felt vulnerable telling her I couldn't pull myself up from the place I was in. Yet, at the same time, I felt hopeful this would be a step in the right direction.

When we arrived in Mexico, I knew something in me would change that week. I prayed it was going to be a good change, but I was pretty jaded from my past experiences. It started rocky. Andy was drinking enough for both of us, so I was both angry and jealous. I felt like I was a single mom, pregnant, and alone with her three kids in a foreign country. It was hard, and for a day or two, I really sulked in my resentment for him and our life. But halfway through the trip, I woke up early one morning and started getting ready for the day before anyone else was up. As I sat in front of the mirror doing my makeup, I had a moment when everything changed.

Have you ever had a moment in which it felt like the light bulb finally turned on? I had been waiting for this one moment for years, and it just happened at the most ordinary time. I often wonder if it was the moment my antidepressant finally kicked in, or if I finally opened my ears and heard what God was speaking to me. It seemed so clear to me at that moment I needed to change. I looked at myself and told myself I couldn't change Andy, I couldn't change our past year, and I couldn't change my pregnancy, but I could change myself. My entire life I had dreamed about having a big family. I wanted four kids! I was living out the biggest and best dream of my entire life, but because the timing wasn't right, or because I couldn't drink, or because people made comments about four kids, or because my marriage wasn't perfect, I wasn't letting myself find joy in any part of it.

The shame suddenly felt ridiculous to me. I was in MEXICO, with my GROWING FAMILY. If I couldn't find joy here, then it would be almost impossible to find it at home.

I sat there and rubbed my growing belly. For the first time, I let myself fall in love with the little girl growing inside of me. And yes, before you try to add that up, that's one boy and THREE girls. When I heard my family begin to rustle around, I took one last look in the mirror and said to myself, *It's time. If you don't feel it, then you fake it until you make it.* And that's what I did.

My kids woke up to a mom who was so full of joy and excitement for the day ahead. Even though Andy was groggy from his hangover, and I wanted to be mad, I kissed him and told him how excited I was. As much as I hated when Andy drank, I pep-talked myself into having a good attitude and finding joy in every moment the best I could. I also gave myself permission to not let his moods and drinking affect me anymore. I wasn't choosing to ignore his problem or condone it now. I was just choosing to focus on myself first. If I was going to try to fix something to make our life better, I needed to be responsible for working on myself before anyone else.

I decided to finally announce my pregnancy. I had my son take a picture of my pregnant belly in front of some Spanish artwork and posted it straight to Facebook. I didn't second guess it or wonder what people would say when they saw "another baby," or "another girl," or how I would feel when people made comments about me always being pregnant, and, "Aren't your hands already full?" It didn't matter what other people thought, and I finally stopped telling myself to get permission from the world to live my own life. My life was going to change. For the first time, I realized God's timing is the right timing. This pregnancy and this baby girl were going to change the course of my life. I wasn't ready for another baby, and I was scared, but the gift of this new life was healing my loss. She came at the perfect time and pushed me to change our future. I was going to do it, even when I didn't feel like it.

When we arrived home from Mexico, I knew my instinct would be to go back to my same depressed state. It was hard to wake up joyful when I was no longer on the coast of Mexico. Instead, I woke up to our normal life in the dead of winter. Nothing had changed in my life on the outside, yet I was still forcing myself to try to change from the inside. I climbed out of bed every morning and told myself to keep on faking it. The work felt excruciating. My instinct was to criticize my husband, to yell at him for drinking, to check out when the sun went down, to focus on the hard and the bad, and to isolate myself from friends and family. I had to deliberately do the opposite of that every single hour of every single day.

There were days I felt like all was hopeless. Some days, I was sure my marriage was too broken, and some days, I felt I was too broken. But I had made a plan that morning in Mexico. I already knew there would be hard days. I knew that because every single day was already hard. I downloaded podcasts, made a play-list, bought books, and had my uplifting friends on speed dial. I knew what it would take to bring me out of a daily funk. I would tell myself each day to just do it today. Make it through today, and tomorrow, if I was in the same mood, I could cry all day. Do you know, though, what happens when you push through a bad moment? Getting through that one circumstance renews your strength to get through another. I would think to myself, "Wow, if I just got through that, I can get through this, too." The goal was never a year of happiness at that point. I just wanted to try every day. I always told myself that tomorrow I could break down, shame-free. But I rarely needed it. The more I pushed through, found moments of joy, and "faked it," the easier it got. I wanted to get to the point I no longer had to fake it; I wanted happiness to be my reality.

Slowly but surely, I did feel happiness again. The summer didn't just bring warmth in the air but warmth in my heart. As I watched my belly grow, I embraced this familiar, exciting, and uncomfortable feeling. I knew this would be the last time I experienced this, so I wanted to find all the joy I could in this season. I often had waves of panic overcome me because I knew that post-partum triggered my spiral last time. I was scared drinking would become my crutch again. I wanted to be as prepared as I could before Remi was born so I would never go back to the place I had worked so hard to escape from. My pregnancy felt like a ticking time bomb. As anxious and excited as I was to meet our last girl, I was afraid I would fail and lose myself again. I knew my family deserved more, and that I deserved more, but sometimes, I let fear overcome me, and I'd ask myself if I was strong enough to give more.

As my pregnancy came to an end, I definitely had days when I let fear win, and I would sob at the possibility of diving back into alcohol and failing my family. But I didn't always let fear win. In fact, I was determined to win. I was determined to have a plan and change this vicious cycle-this cycle of hurting, coping in the wrong way, and ignoring the problem. It was a generational cycle that started long before I was born—even before my mom. She witnessed the cycle, then became a part of it, and I had witnessed it and had become part of it too. Now that I was aware of it, I realized how much I did not want this cycle to continue for more generations to come. I was determined I was going to end this *right now*, with me.

Why Does This Even Matter?

Addiction is real, you guys. I know everyone knows it is real, but it often seems like it only happens to "other people" and involves hard drugs. But the reality is, for most people, it creeps into their lives and presents itself as harmless and fun, yet develops into everything except that. Maybe because this was my own vice, but I feel like alcohol addiction is tricky. I often looked to others for some kind of comparison to see if what I was doing was too much or too often, and honestly, I didn't find anyone telling me it was. I saw and knew lots of people doing the exact same thing I was doing. Everywhere on social media and out and about, I saw alcohol. I even still regularly see memes of a coffee cup passing a torch to a glass of wine. *It seems so normal.*

The more I think about it, the more I am sure it isn't exclusive to alcohol. Every single day someone gets prescribed pain pills. I see it daily because I work in healthcare. I know firsthand that patients come in with legitimate pain. Eventually, for some people, the *desire* for more pain pills outweighs the *need* to control the pain. But just like in my example with alcohol, turning to the public for comparison is futile because so many people are using pain pills to cover up more than just physical pain. To them, it seems so normal. Addiction is a broad term that can truly be applied to almost everything from exercise to heroin, but it all starts from an unmet desire. When our desires are being met with this "substance" or "thing," even momentarily, it becomes a crutch we fall back on in times of desperation. For me, my crutch became a lifeline, and I felt like I needed the alcohol more than I didn't.

I am writing this book to help someone in need. I am writing everything I needed someone to tell me as I was going through every stage of my life. The tricky part about this particular part of the lesson, though, is I can't teach someone how to look into their heart and realize they have a problem. I am going to assume that if you have the courage to grab a self-help book off of the shelf, you can probably do some soul-searching and honestly tell yourself when you have a problem. But this part right here; this is where people stop, right after the comparison I described above.

Just like my example: I looked around to see if what I was doing was outside of the norm, and when it wasn't, I kept doing the very thing I should've stopped. You can't let yourself stop after you look around for comparison. I promise you, if you are looking for someone worse off than you to use as a comparison to where you are, you will absolutely find it. Don't stop there. Go deeper than that. *Own up*. Does this feel right to you? If it truly does feel right, you wouldn't have to even ask yourself this question. So many people don't even let themselves get to the question of if it feels right in their heart because the answer is more than they're willing to accept and work through.

When I finally got out of the comparison trap that justified every choice I made, I was left with something much harder than I wanted to deal with. My life felt meaningless. I was tired, I was sad, and I was waking up with regret day after day. I realized I could look around at friends, the public, and social media all I wanted for the answer as to whether I had an alcohol addiction or not, but it didn't really matter if my heart was telling me I did. Owning up was hard to do. Once I stopped comparing myself to those who were worse off than myself, I had to admit I had a problem. I didn't have a ton of apologizing to do to people around me because I hid so much of my drinking and grief. But I knew I hadn't been showing up as my best self for years, and everyone around me deserved better. I owed it to everyone that had been showing up for me when I wasn't showing up for them: my husband, my kids, my mom, my aunt, my in-laws, and my friends. I had no one to blame but myself for my decisions, and now it was left up to only me to make it right. I had to own up to my mom and apologize for not showing sympathy during the years she struggled. As hard as owning up is, it changes everything.

There are people out there who won't ever break out of the comparison trap and won't understand when you do. To hold a mirror up to your own life and change a bad habit inadvertently holds a mirror up to those around you who haven't changed yet. As much as you want those people to support you, expect pushback and questions. Your job isn't to convince anyone else to change. Your job is to change yourself. Can you let yourself listen to that pulling in your heart telling you this isn't right, even though everyone around you is saying it is normal? You honestly can't take on any truths of this book until you understand that comparison isn't your guiding tool. God is your guiding tool. The unsettled feeling in your heart is. Your peace and happiness is. Everyone else is just a spectator. They don't get a say unless they are fighting your battle with you.

Overcoming addiction: As a disclaimer, my story is mine, and I am giving you all of the tools I used. I feel that—given my family history and the circumstances surrounding my addiction—I got out fast, and I was truly lucky. I am giving you the tools to identify your strongholds. These will help you identify triggers and overcome them. Sometimes the cycle can end with controlling your triggers, but so often, it doesn't. If what you are dealing with is a true addiction, please seek professional help. Addiction steals so much from lives every day. If you feel your addiction lies deeper than what I write about (overcoming triggers), then please seek professionals. As much as I believe this book will help you, I do not underestimate the value of true, consistent, professional help. Seek the professionals to overcome something many people never do. You have people who love you, and we are all rooting for you.

Your life matters.

Now we are moving on to the life application for this chapter. Buckle up. This one is hard.

Life application for this chapter:

Step 1: Identify Your Triggers.

I feel like this step could be the easiest step if you pay attention to yourself. Every time you reach for your addiction—whether it's bolting out of the door for a run, grabbing a candy bar, or chugging that glass of wine—stop yourself right then. Spend a few minutes, and if you can, write down what it is you are feeling and what is specifically triggering it. According to James Clear in his NY Times bestseller, Atomic Habits, there are typically five "triggers" that lead to both good and bad habits.[4]

1. Time
2. Location
3. Preceding Event
4. Emotional State
5. Other People

Identifying when, or what specific triggers lead us to our methods of coping will allow us the power to prepare for them and change them. Spend a week or two making a note every single time you reach for your "crutch," to identify what you are feeling right before you get to the point of needing your "fix." Knowing your triggers puts the power back into your own hands. James Clear states in his book a bad habit

MENDED

is not undone, it is replaced. If you know what leads to your coping method, then you are able to prepare for those triggers ahead of time.

Step 2: Prepare for your triggers to happen

From the very first day Andy brought home the bottle of wine until the day we were taking shots at a birthday party, I was looking for one thing: relief. Life was hard. The thing is, I always knew it was going to be hard. I had gone through hard times, and I had accepted every one of those experiences as opportunities to grow; even the untimely death of my grandma. Hard doesn't just happen to some people; it happens to every single one of us. I knew this truth. But when the pain came in the form of three crazy kids and a grief that creeped in many months after the death, it was a surprise. I hadn't prepared for it to feel the way it did. I realize now I had always had triggers, but I had been better prepared for them.

If you documented when you were triggered, as I described above, you probably found some type of pattern. Now that you know what your triggered feelings are, what can you do to prepare for them in advance? I wake up early to have my own special time to myself, so I feel refreshed before my kids get up and everything gets crazy. It helps me feel in control of my day and my emotions.

Your trigger could be loneliness. When you know you will be alone for a while, can you call a parent or friend to chat for a few minutes? What about feeling triggered when anxious for your spouse to come home? That used to be mine too. What about calling them to chat on their way home? I call my husband and give him a heads up about the state of the kids, our house, my mood, ask him how he's feeling, and about his day before he ever walks into the door. That preparation gives us both some insight on how to deal with each other more gracefully than if we didn't know. Everyday triggers like stress, boredom, anxiousness, and loneliness are easy to identify but hard to break. Why? Because they happen every single day, and you must have a real plan in place to successfully break these. Once you have logged your feelings for a week or two, go back and formulate three to five things that would have helped you feel better right at that moment to replace your typical crutch. Stick it to your refrigerator, if food is your problem, or to the bottle of wine if that's your issue. Prepare yourself in advance. Have a plan!

Step 3: Seek professional help

I know for a lot of people, this isn't really the advice that you want. Therapy may be a necessity. For starters, what if your trigger is abandonment? Abuse? Death? There are many steps you may be able to take, like I mentioned, to redirect you in times when you are reaching for your addiction, but you have to get to the root of your pain if you want to stand a chance to completely recover. Pushing it to the back of your mind, while you call a friend or take a hot bath might work for a while, but true healing is a process that professionals are trained to unpack, evaluate, and walk you through.

I didn't go to therapy, right away, for my depression that led to alcohol dependency, but I did seek professional help. The day I told my doctor what I was feeling, I felt like the weight on my shoulders had been lifted. Someone finally knew, and I wouldn't have to carry this burden alone. That alone felt like I could get through this. Life isn't simply about surviving. You were made to THRIVE. Sometimes, therapy or medication is that first step to doing more than just surviving. Whatever you choose, be proud you made that first hard step to a better life.

Step 4: Find Accountability.

Accountability is a game-changer. Having an actual person who knows your struggles, won't judge, and keeps you "in check" when you want to steer off course, can be life-changing. It was for me because I knew I couldn't do it alone. I knew I would always find some excuse to choose my bad habit over my good. My husband and a good friend are my accountability partners. I had to let them into my struggles and tell them how serious I was about changing my life. I had to ask them to step in and hold me accountable for the promises I had made myself, even if it made them feel awkward to tell me a hard truth if the time came.

People don't like overstepping boundaries, so you might have to tell them why it is so important to you. Once I did this, I felt prepared to live this life to the best of my ability. I had a team on my side. Because of that, I feel so much stronger than I have ever been. There are still days where I feel weak. As I am writing this, we are on lockdown because of COVID at our house, and I am homeschooling my children for the first time ever. I. AM. TRIGGERED. I need relief. Last night, I had convinced myself it was finally an appropriate time for a glass of wine (or two). Maybe it was. That would have been nice.

I quickly texted my husband and a friend to see what they thought, and because I had made them my accountability partners, they did exactly what I had asked. They held me accountable. They asked the hard questions, "Is this because you are wanting a relaxing night or because you are triggered and need an escape?" and "Don't you have a run planned for tomorrow?" Because of their feedback, I was able to reconsider *why* I wanted a drink, and I ultimately decided not to.

Having them by my side almost feels like another form of therapy. Their willingness to pay attention to my habits and their bravery to tell me the truth, even when it might hurt, is an irreplaceable gift in my life. I encourage you to find someone who will do that for you. You should never have to fight your battles alone.

Step 5: Replace Your Bad Habit with a Good Habit.

For me, this step took some time. As much as I wanted to stop my bad habits, whether it was binge eating or having wine, it was hard to replace those bad habits in the moment. I had myself conditioned to think these things were the only thing that cured my anxiety. It took time for me to figure out something else I could replace my habits with. To do this, you have to find something you enjoy but also something important enough to you to keep doing it. For my husband, it became working out and going to the shooting range. These provided the stress relief he needed, and with both, he set goals that he wanted to accomplish. This made it such that he wanted to keep going to achieve that goal.

This book and running became my replacements. I use those things to replace my triggers, and now those things hold me accountable during times I would normally reach for a drink. I wake up at 5:30 a.m. to write and/or to run. Knowing I have something important or fulfilling to my life or something fun to do early the next day reminds me that picking up a drink and ruining it just isn't worth it. If I am being honest, I feel like getting to that mentality, that running and writing were better than a drink, took time. I was constantly second-guessing my decision and having to intentionally choose to make a good decision time and time again. That is when your accountability partner also helps.

Having a new hobby truly felt like the last crucial piece I needed to change my habits and my life. You can track your triggers and figure out what causes them, but without having something that makes you *want* to say *no*, it makes it pretty hard to not give in. I encourage you to find something in your life as well, that makes you want to give up whatever negative habit it is that you are fighting. It isn't easy. This work took time. One step at a time, one day at a time, one good decision after another is what will change your life.

This is hard stuff, you guys. It is. I pray for every single person who reads this, that my words pierce your heart and help you find hope for a better tomorrow. This work took me years. It wasn't easy, but dang, *it was so worth it.* Each step was crucial. If I had never listened to the unsettled feeling in my heart, looked beyond that comparison trap, figured out what triggered me, sought help, found accountability, and replaced my habit, I wouldn't be living out my dreams today. Just sitting here typing this book is a dream I never ever thought was possible. It actually wouldn't have been possible had I not gone through the work.

Do the work.

Don't fall into the comparison trap. Fall into the trap of being the best version of yourself every single day. The possibilities for your life are endless. As long as you are on this earth breathing, God has a plan for you. Break out of those habits, and work to achieve that plan. I promise you, it is worth it.

Eight

KNOW WHEN TO CHANGE
& WHEN TO FORGIVE

I had known for a while, but Andy had been struggling with alcohol just like me. After all, we were drinking together for almost two years. I guess that is when many people start to struggle and have a "quarter-life" crisis. Life gets hard, and there are big decisions to make. We were in our mid-to-late twenties when life started to get tough. I was so consumed with losing my grandma, my third pregnancy, and raising our children, that I didn't see Andy was struggling with the same things I was. He was also devastated by the loss of my grandmother, he was nervous about having another baby, and he was having some big changes in his career. For so long, I thought I was the only one struggling, and I just pulled him along. Really, he was on his way before I ever realized it.

Two years prior, one day before Eden (our third baby) was due, and just two months after my grandma passed away, I noticed Andy's drinking for the first time. I was at home, busy prepping last-minute items for the hospital stay and delivery. Our relationship was fine at the time, but we were both grieving and keeping ourselves busy, which made our marriage a little stale. When I found Andy to get him to pack up the car, I noticed he was not himself. He was stumbling and slurring. He reeked of liquor. This day was the first day I experienced him drinking outside of a social setting. I was confused. The more I tried to get him to focus, the more aggravated he got with me. When I stopped asking questions, he seemed to get it together and finished helping me pack the car. I was relieved for a minute, until he stopped what he was doing, turned around, looked me in the eyes, and said, "I want a divorce."

A day before our third child was to come into the world.

I felt the blood instantly drain from my body. *What, how...why? We were fine yesterday!* I felt the panic overtake me. I called my sister-in-law and cried as I questioned what to do. She calmed me down, suggested he needed to sleep it off, and reassured me he did not mean any of it. I did what she said and waited until he went to bed. When he was asleep, I shut myself in the baby's nursery and sobbed. This was not how I'd envisioned the birth of our third child.

Andy woke up the next day feeling groggy and remorseful. He wanted to apologize for the way he'd acted, but I couldn't even think about the day before when I had so much ahead for me on this day. I needed this day to be what I dreamed it would be—the calm after my storm. I focused on my labor and delivery and tried to forget about the day before. The birth of Eden was beautiful and special just like I had envisioned. His remorse didn't fade, and he showed me through words and action during the following weeks and months how much he didn't mean what he had said. But for me, that memory stuck. It was my first glimpse into his struggle with alcohol.

Over the next two years, in the time between my last two pregnancies, there were a lot of instances where I could sense he was losing control of his drinking. It was never the same as the first time because he never again mentioned divorce, but the more alcohol he consumed, the more different his demeanor became. Normally confident, silly, and almost overly loving, with alcohol, he was insecure, irritated, and ill-mannered.

When I got pregnant with our last baby and started my process of healing and growth from grief, stress, and my own alcohol problem, I gained clarity about his problem. I could tell he was losing himself. I desperately tried to pull him up with me to no avail. Because I was no longer drinking and was now working through the process of figuring out my triggers, I saw how damaging alcohol could be to a person and a family. It changes you. It brought out the worst in Andy.

The closer we got to having our last baby, the more stressed he was. The more responsibility he had at work, the more insecure he felt. The wilder the kids were, the more irritated he got. The more stressed, insecure, and irritated he felt, the more he drank. He tried hard not to drink every day, but when he did drink, he drank a lot, and all of his feelings came out. It broke my heart to watch because each time I could see it happening. I could see the insecurity, hurt, and stress in his eyes. I could feel it. We all could. I just didn't know how to fix it when he was trying to fix it himself in all of the wrong ways. Slowly, my resentment toward him started to grow. It had been two years since I first noticed this change in him, and now I was feeling pretty angered by it.

The cycle was exhausting. He would wake up with regret because he hated the way he'd acted when drinking, which would cause his insecurity and self-loathing, which led to more drinking. Once he started drinking, I would start panicking. I could feel his mood changing with every sip he took. Those nights were starting to add up in my head. The minutes he spent drinking instead of playing with the kids were minutes I counted up: hating the time lost and hating him for it. The situation felt hopeless. Every morning, he would wake up and say he hated himself but didn't know how to change. The answer was obvious, but confessing you have a problem seemed even worse. I kept holding out hope that he would change as soon as the baby was born. That had always seemed to be a turning point in our life.

Unlike my previous pregnancy and delivery that was calm and exciting, this one was the opposite. I don't know if it was because our home life wasn't ideal or if I just had fears about a delivery, but I was scared. I felt unsure walking into the hospital that morning. Not that I was ever thinking of walking into the experience of birthing a child and expecting it to be "easy," but I thought I knew what to expect. This day felt different from the start. I woke up feeling uneasy. I opened up a book of Bible scriptures, and I told Andy I wanted to just flip to a random one and hope it had the encouragement I needed. I flipped my book open to a page with the words, "He who believes in me, though he may die, he shall live" (John 11:25, ESV). "Well," I thought to myself as I broke down in tears, "that wasn't the encouragement I wanted for today." Andy saw my fear and reminded me of my other deliveries that were all relatively flawless. I knew he was right, but my anxiousness increased the closer we got to the hospital.

The labor was anything but easy. It seemed to be moving quickly, but the pain was excruciating. It was an unfamiliar feeling. My previous unmedicated births were painful, but I had managed to talk myself through the pain. For some reason, I couldn't get through this pain. I stopped pushing, and I pleaded for the doctors to make it stop. The pain was more intense than it had been for any of my other births, and I thought I couldn't handle it. After what felt like hours,

Remi finally came, and I scooped her up and held her close. I looked into her eyes and felt gutted with overwhelming love. I apologized to her for being scared and unhappy at first and promised her a life full of love.

Our moment was special, however, it was very brief. As I was holding her, I could feel something unusual happening. I immediately felt the nurse scoop up Remi, pass her to Andy, and come rushing back to me. I had started to hemorrhage. The hour that followed was terrifying. The doctors and nurses were running around, pushing on my body, and administering different medications into my IV. When I asked if I would be okay, no one said *yes*. The blood was unrelenting, and I could see the panic in the nurses' faces. I tried to stay calm, but inside I was petrified. I stared across the room at Andy and my mom, feeling like it was the last time I would ever see them. I hadn't told them I loved them. I thought about my babies at home. I thought about who would dance with my son at his wedding, who would do my daughters' hair on the first day of school, and our new daughter's first birthday party. Those were the things I wanted to see. The nurses pushed, called for backup, and ran around more. The situation was intense, and everyone in the room was diligently working to save my life. In an instant, everyone and everything just stopped. My nurse looked at me, exhausted, and told me I had severely hemorrhaged, but it was finally over.

Just like that.

The experience of that delivery shook me to the core. I cried during the entire hospital stay. I was so thankful to be alive, but I felt like I was made aware of how fragile life is in the worst way. I felt like God was teaching me a lesson, and quite frankly I did not like the way it was presented. But to be fair, I think I needed it. I had done the hard work and coached myself throughout my pregnancy regarding how to get to a better place mentally, but I knew I was scared going into delivery because I didn't trust myself to not give in to my negative behaviors. After the hemorrhage, however, I was no longer scared I would fail at it. I had been scared almost to death. I was not going to waste my life again. What I was really afraid of this time was how I would feel doing it *alone*.

After that experience, I came home from the hospital a changed person. I didn't talk to Andy about how that experience changed me. I no longer cared what he did. He would do what he wanted anyway. I cared about myself and how I could make it through every day a better person. At first, I had Andy by my side. Creating a new life is such a sobering experience, and for a little bit, I felt like maybe this was the wake-up call he was waiting on. Unfortunately, though, our newborn bliss only lasted for as long as my maternity leave. His drinking slowly and consistently began to increase. I was frustrated and emotionally spent.

My whole life I felt like I was trying to save my mom from her addiction to no avail. With my addiction, no one saved me. I had to make the decision to change and do it myself. Now, here he was, addicted but with no desire to change on his own. I was tired of doing all of the work. I couldn't keep saving someone who never wanted to be saved. It truly felt like I was jumping in the water to save him from drowning, but instead of grabbing the life raft, he just continued to drown. Exhausted, my only option would be to leave and save myself or drown too. Either way, I would lose something.

After several months of witnessing his continual drinking, I gave in too. Eventually, I started drinking *with* him in an attempt to numb what I didn't want to feel. The first time I woke up with a hangover and that familiar shameful, hopeless feeling, I ended the cycle for myself. I decided I could not drown with him. I had to remember my near-death experience, remember my children, and remember my future. I had to step out of the water and save myself. But that meant leaving him in the water. I had to set rules and boundaries that prevented me from drowning with him. It felt cruel to let him feel the consequences of his mistakes, but it was so necessary. He began to understand when he realized our bedroom door was locked or the kids and I did not come home if I knew he was drinking. He finally realized alcohol was impacting our family. He asked me if we could go to therapy together-something he had never considered before.

Therapy began when we needed it the most. It was intense and made us both take responsibility for our problems. Our therapist coached us on moving forward without holding on to bad habits. It seemed to be impossible to remove alcohol from our life without replacing it with something better. After a few sessions of therapy, Andy and I seriously committed to change. Uncomfortable change. We were at the end of our rope of unhappiness. Our family was everything that we'd ever dreamed of. We had too many good and beautiful times together to ruin it with drunken nights and mean words. We promised we would make uncomfortable decisions, one after another until we could find our way out of this mess. It was one of the most serious, consistent, and life-changing decisions we ever made.

Together, we found a new church to go to. We had completely stopped going to church after my grandma had died (not for any reason particularly), and we wanted to start fresh. We searched until we found a small church that had big dreams to change the world. A church that loved God and took you in exactly as you were. It was uncomfortable enough to walk into a crowded place full of strangers, but as soon as we did that, we did even more. We signed up to take classes to grow-ones where we would have to be vulnerable, speak out loud, and share our weaknesses with people around us. It felt so wild and unfamiliar to me but exhilarating. Slowly, I could see him breaking free from the cycle of alcohol addiction he was in. We were having more good nights than bad nights. The drinking was minimal. We were talking again. We were kissing again. Our kids were watching us laugh together and laughed too. It felt like we had finally found the way out.

As much as our life was improving, it still felt like there was a huge elephant in the room. Andy still drank, just not as often. Even though it was rare to see his unpleasant side when he drank, it would still rear its ugly head and destroy our hard work time and time again. We were on a break from therapy, too, our only accountability. Without it, the drinking slowly increased again. I was in a place where I was holding on to so much anxiety and resentment towards him because every day felt like a ticking time bomb. I was constantly on edge because, even though it was less often, I never knew when he would be drinking or what his mood would be when he did.

Our marriage would ultimately crumble if we didn't eliminate both the cause of this (alcohol) and the resentment I was holding on to. We decided together, through many conversations and tears, we had to make a necessary step for the sake of our marriage and family. For him, it would be to give up alcohol completely. For me, it would be to forgive completely. Forgiveness has been an everyday process for me. At first, it was trusting that he would change. Then, it was working through fears of what our future would look like. In the present, forgiveness presents itself as a hope for the future, without the constant reminder of our past. Forgiveness as a couple means to show up and do the uncomfortable work every single day.

This week marks two years of sobriety for my husband. He hasn't had an irrational moment since he put down the bottle. Not to say there aren't hard moments or arguments, though. Marriage is an assiduously hard job in itself, even without the alcohol. Since quitting, he has lost thirty pounds, looks better than ever, and he has found new hobbies like fishing, hunting, and lifting weights. His happiness radiates, our kids cling to him like he is Superman, and I am more in love and proud of him than I have ever been of anyone in my entire life. He did the hard, uncomfortable work, and he saved his life and our family.

Why Does This Even Matter?

Acceptance is hard. Change is hard. Forgiveness is hard. This chapter is hard. I hated watching Andy go through this. I hated it even more because he was walking such a thin line with me. On one side, I was angry, protective of our family, and fed up with his drunken shenanigans. On the other side, I knew who he was sober, and I knew that person was good. I also knew who he was drunk, and even though he was mean, I could see the hurt and insecurity in his eyes. It was a painful rollercoaster ride that we were on.

The year and a half-ish that I was on my "finding myself or finding happiness" journey and Andy was on his downward spiral, I started understanding things I had been trying to understand my entire life. It wasn't necessarily about addiction, abuse, or growth; although, those were all things I was getting oddly comfortable tackling. It was about relationships. Anytime I had a problem or situation in a relationship, whether that was between my mom, my ex-boyfriend, or my friends, I was able to take it for what it was. What I mean is, I could have a problem in one relationship without it affecting any other relationship. I knew people acted differently, and just because I was having an issue with one person did not mean it applied to all of the other relationships in my life.

Somehow, though, as I walked through this time with Andy, all of those lines were blurred for me. It was almost like PTSD from my mom's addiction. Maybe, because I loved both my mom and Andy unconditionally, I held them both to a high standard of expectations in my head. I wanted my love to be reciprocated. Anytime Andy was drunk, I was immediately thrown back to being a high schooler and arguing with my mom who was high on drugs. The feeling of abandonment swept over me, and it somehow triggered my troubled feelings towards my mom. Also, when I would see my mom, and she would be acting drunk, I became upset with both her *and* Andy. It would always catch him off-guard, and he would be standing there asking me what he was doing wrong, but I couldn't explain it.

I was just so angry he and my mom could put me through this grueling cycle simultaneously. Knowing I was "looking after" two people on separate paths of addiction felt too much to take on, although neither had asked me to take it on. I thought that would end as soon as he stopped drinking, but the problem was that it didn't. I continuously lumped him in with any hurt I felt. I just couldn't understand why I was asked to bear a burden that felt larger than I could handle, even as he was in recovery.

This chapter's life application isn't something you can do in just one day. It is continuous work that has to be done daily, unceasingly, all the days of your life, if you want full freedom and to feel full forgiveness towards a person. It has taken me almost a full two years into Andy's recovery to understand these truths and to walk them out. Once I did, our relationship suddenly seemed to shift into love and growth instead of the path of just survival. As you are walking through hurt but ready to forgive people in your life, these are the steps that could help.

Life application for this chapter:

Step 1: Set Boundaries.

We have all heard of boundaries. More specifically, do we set the right boundaries in the right relationships? How necessary are boundaries?

I immediately looked to the Bible for thoughts on this, and honestly, what I found was so conflicting. First, I found, "for each one should carry their own load" (Galatians 6:5, NIV). Then I found, "Seldom set foot in your neighbor's house-too much of you, and they will hate you." (Proverbs 25:17, NIV). I liked both of these verses because they confirmed what I had already wanted and what I had learned. I wanted to wash my hands clean of their problems and be done. I wanted to let them "bear [their] own load." I had already done my work; now it was their turn. I also saw Proverbs 25:17 come to life for me firsthand. The more I dug in, got angry, and tried to "help" or change them, the more they distanced themselves from me and disliked me for it. Those verses confirmed to me that I should just stay out of their problems and whatever consequences came, it was on them.

But right as I got comfortable accepting that, I stumbled on scripture that read, "Rescue those who are being taken away to death; hold back those who are stumbling to the slaughter" (Proverbs 24:11, ESV). I didn't understand how to do both. How do I rescue someone but also let them bear their own burdens? How was it possible to do both? That is when I discovered boundaries. Alas, you can love and protect yourself *and* help your drowning loved ones. Setting boundaries with Andy presumably saved our marriage. I realized after many arguments and apologies that something wasn't working.

The cycle was continuous and relentless. Mess up, argue, apologize, change behavior for a week, mess up again, then start the cycle again. I realized rescuing someone didn't mean to drown in the process. Sometimes it meant to hand him the life raft and swim away to safety. Each time he messed up, there were boundaries set. Honestly, I hated it because to me, it seemed like I was parenting him, even though we'd decided on the boundaries together. Ultimately, the boundaries saved our family. I can't tell you that it was easy or quick because it wasn't. We had to work through and create new boundaries every step of the way. When we realized one wasn't working, we readjusted. The boundaries created weren't to punish anyone, but they were in place to protect him, me, and our children.

I have had to place boundaries in my life with many people for many reasons, including myself. The problem doesn't have to be dangerously destructive like mine or my husband's alcoholism. It is important to know, in every situation, where you stand, what you are willing to take, and what the result is if the line is crossed. It could be someone's negativity, your child's tantrums, or your mom's comments on how to parent. I have spoken with other people who have set boundaries, and here are a few of their examples:

- No TV time if you continue to make a mess.
- When your mom comments on your parenting, politely

tell her you're parenting differently. If she continues to comment, the visits will be shorter or less frequent to protect yourself from that condemnation.

- If a friend pressures you to drink or makes comments about the fact you don't, decline opportunities to hang out in settings where alcohol is present.
- If a friend is negative, let them know you can not take on the daily negativity. Venting is okay, but daily negativity about everything will end the friendship.

Don't get it confused. Boundaries aren't meant to parent someone and to give consequences for bad behavior. Boundaries create environments that are comfortable for all parties involved. If someone doesn't know their boundary with you or doesn't know something that bothers you, the chances of them stopping that behavior (at least around you) is pretty slim. With boundaries, there isn't confusion about expectations and wishes because they are stated and known.

Boundaries let love flourish.

Because of boundaries, you know what to expect from relationships. Boundaries are the platform on which great, long, healthy relationships are built.

Step 2: Accept that their path may look different than yours.

One year ago, I was angry. I felt like I should be happy or relieved at least. Andy had just committed to a lifelong promise he would never drink again. It was different than before. Previously, he would promise to change the result of his drunkenness: the anger. Now, he was changing the cause: the alcohol. He had even gone further and gotten to the root of the problem through therapy: his insecurity. But I wasn't happy or relieved. I was more than angry. I was furious.

I had already been working on myself for a year at this point. I felt strong in the changes I had made and who I was becoming. On top of that, we have four children. Our oldest was eight years old. Smart and a daddy's boy, he needed Andy to shape up and be his best self-to be an example. But Andy just couldn't do it for years. Or if he could have, he chose not to. Those things made me mad. Pregnancy had changed me. A near-death experience changed me. Our complete family changed me. Therapy changed me. Church changed me. Reading certain books changed me. *Why weren't those same things changing him, too?*

I resented the fact that he needed outside resources and to be on the brink of divorce to finally get his act together. If I'm being really honest, I also hated the way he made me question my decisions too. He committed to never drinking a drink again, while I still liked to have a glass of wine every now and then. Did that make me a bad person now too? I didn't like it. I often got angry and asked him why it had to get to this point for him to realize he needed to change? Why did he have to flip our entire world upside down to finally put the drink down?

I know some people might not understand this because maybe you feel like this isn't the truth. I think it is. *His recovery was none of my business.* It affected me, yes. It affected our family, absolutely. However, we are not the same person. What triggers me doesn't trigger him. What I needed to make a change wasn't what he needed. As much as it hurts to realize this, it is a fact. Some people need a family talk or the birth of a new baby, while other people need AA meetings and therapy to change. Some people need major consequences to see what their actions have caused. God made each of us unique. We all know that. If our hair, skin, laughs, and talents are all unique, why wouldn't our roads to recovery also be unique? When I finally stopped asking why his road to recovery was so different from mine and just accepted he had decided to change and that this is what worked for him, I was able to move on to forgiving him.

Step 3: Fully Forgive

Forgive: verb

To cease to feel resentment against (an offender): PARDON

To give up resentment of or claim to requital

To cancel (a debt)

To grant relief from a payment of[5]

I have to say, I could not have even attempted this step without successfully understanding step two. Step two is crucial. Once I was able to get through that, I was able to open my eyes to a world of forgiveness. Not only for Andy, but for any person I had held some type of resentment towards, big or small. I personally like the definition of forgive: to cancel. To cancel something out completely means it didn't happen. You cancel a transaction at a store, you get your money back. You leave with the same amount of money you started with. When I think of it that way, to cancel a debt means I love my husband, my mom, that friend, just the same as I did before. I treat them the way I did before. While I know relationships change, and some relationships, you have to let go of, I am referring to people who made a mistake and have changed.

I think of forgiveness in two ways. First, it lets the person walk through life without dragging their past behind them. I saw this sometimes with my mom, I see it in myself, and I see it in Andy. If the past gets brought up, there is suddenly a change in mood. Andy gets sad. I am filled with shame. My mom gets defensive. No one benefits from reliving a past mistake. It is a weight that slows a person down and often has them looking back. The more a person is assured that their past is gone, the less that shame consumes them, and the more they grow from it. They get to live a life of freedom. They don't have to carry that extra load with them.

The second thing about forgiveness, and what I think is the most important, is what happens within your own heart. Christian author Lewis B. Smedes said, "To forgive is to set a prisoner free and discover that the prisoner was you."[6] How real is that? What does holding on to other people's mistakes do for you? It weighs you down and breeds anger. Without forgiveness, the past never actually gets left in the past. It becomes a tool to manipulate. It creates anger and shame. It can cause the other person to question why they even changed if nothing positive came from it. I know this because I was that person. I have to repeat to myself when I get caught in the spiral of what someone else has done, that it was never about me.

The mean words, the abandonment, the gossip: it was never about you. It was about the other person not knowing how to work through their troubles. If you hold on to those negative insults towards you, you start to believe them. Even if you never get an official apology from a person, you have to free yourself from their actions. Cancel out that debt so *you* can live with a joyful heart. Forgiveness isn't forgetting and losing boundaries. Forgiveness is for you. Let it go. Free your heart, mind, and life.

Nine

MENDING.

Here we are. The last chapter. At first, this chapter was titled "Mended," just like the title of the book. But the more I looked at it, the more it felt like the title implied the hard work was over. It implies this book is a neatly packaged gift to you with the instructions, "Follow these nine chapters, and you will earn yourself a fairytale ending." However, I know it isn't that easy or that neat. It is a process that can sometimes be never-ending. We can always be "mending" ourselves. Just like I learned with heartache and tragedy, you can go through it once, and even though it feels like you deserve a break, you can be dealt the same hand again and again. Putting in the work doesn't mean your circumstances will change into something greater and better. It *will* mean you are better equipped for whatever hardships come your way. Even better than that, though, putting in the effort to learn through each chapter will help you change your perspective. Having a positive perspective gives you the drive to get through any day with a lasting joy in your heart that sadness, bad days, heartache, or negative people can never steal.

Walking with Andy through his journey taught me more than I ever really expected it to. To be honest, there have been very few times in my life I have seen someone change their behavior on my behalf. I feel like I have always been a forgiving person. I have moved on from my past hurts and continued to love the people who intentionally or unintentionally caused pain. But as I walked through his recovery with him, I realized maybe I held on *just a little bit* to some past hurts. Maybe I used my pain as an excuse to be stand-offish or reserved. Maybe I used my painful past as a reason not to reach out or check on people I had said I had forgiven.

As Andy's life began to change, I became aware of the implications of not forgiving and also the freedom when we do. I learned, just as we all did in the last chapter, that to fully forgive means to not hold onto or bring up the past. It was difficult at first. I wanted to blame my bad moods on him sometimes, but I just couldn't. That's when it hit me that maybe it was time to hold *myself* accountable for my actions instead of just shrugging them off as a result of something negative in my past. For the first time, I realized it was *me* who was causing my bad mood, not my circumstances. It wasn't because of my mom's attempted suicide, a breakup, an abortion, my mom's addiction, growing up without a dad, my husband's alcoholism, or my alcoholism. Shifting the mentality that I was in charge of my happiness, no matter what the past held, was a liberating feeling. If I couldn't blame my past, and if my attitude was now based on my own choice, well then, I had to get it together.

The problem with changing your mind is that it takes work *every single day, forever.* When I started writing this book, I thought it would be all you would need to have in your pocket for a perfect life. I believed that once you worked through all of these chapters, life would be exponentially better. It only seems fair that after nine chapters of reliving the past hurt and preparing for the future, one would be able to finally reap the rewards of this changed life. I believed all of that until I sat down and wrote this book. Each chapter is a piece of my life I have been working through, understanding, and growing from for ten years now. But even after a decade of work and writing a book about overcoming your hurdles, I am still finding ways I can improve. I am still fighting the negative-mindset urge consistently. It stems from a deep-rooted belief I once had, and even though I have acknowledged it, I still have to learn from it, and eventually be able to change.

For so long, I have had this belief in my head. I believed this was just my life. I wasn't special, therefore, I could never become something better than what I already was. I believed I was broken and unloved. I had come to accept that and be okay with it. I believed my mistakes absolutely defined who I was, no matter if I changed or if I regretted them. My past life was so wrapped up in shame, I thought once everyone found out about the real me, they would hate me for it. With every wrong decision I make, from snapping at my husband to telling a white lie to a friend, that shame walks right back up to me and gently takes my hand again. For years, when shame took my hand, I would embrace it like we were long-lost friends. I'd hold close to it, almost finding comfort, knowing that no matter what I did to change, I could never truly be someone who was good. It wasn't until I walked through forgiving Andy that I began to realize forgiveness was also something I could offer myself.

Forgiveness is a daily practice for me. Every single day, shame attempts to walk up and take my hand. Slowly, I have learned to shrug it off, push it away, and tell it to leave. It has taken me a long time to get here. I knew I wanted to share the hard stuff with you, but I never in a million years thought I would share *all* of the shameful stuff with you. But as each chapter passed, I felt like the more I wrote about it, the harder it got for shame to take hold of my hand. It is out there in the world, and there is nothing I can do to hide it away in secret in my heart. There's no dark secret tucked away and no invisible handcuffs holding me back from the world. Shame doesn't get to take my hand. You get all of me now.

When I realized shame wasn't supposed to be part of my story, I started making moves. If anything, let that be your one takeaway from the book.

Shame isn't supposed to be part of your story.

Your life, however messed up it may have been, can still be good. I'll forever be thankful to Andy. Because he changed, I learned to forgive. Because I learned to forgive, I realized I could forgive myself and everything that happened to me and because of me. I don't want you to have to wait for someone else to change to see that. If you read this book and do the work, you will know you were made for so much more than to live in the past.

Growth starts small, and you have built up from it almost daily. If I can move on from my past, you can too. Releasing shame from my life gave me opportunities to welcome new things. My growth started as little goals that I mentioned in previous chapters. I had to pick up what was broken and mend my life, health, and relationships back together, piece by piece. What was once a resentful marriage turned into active forgiveness (still not perfect forgiveness). Active forgiveness turned into intentional nightly conversations, which turned into a genuine regained friendship, which turned into a renewed intimacy.

Once I began to forgive myself, I started looking less in the past and more at my future to evaluate my life and priorities. I made health a priority and committed to running just a little bit each week. After literally being unable to run around the block, now I am running half marathons. Mending your life is an intentional choice that has to be made every day, all while pushing shame to the side.

I have yelled at my kids for spilled milk, and before, I would sit in the regret of that burst of anger for hours. To mend your life doesn't mean things aren't broken or that you aren't still breaking things. Because, let's be honest, sometimes I still regretfully yell at my kids. Yelling at my kids seems a little bit like breaking a window. Living life unmended is the mentality that once a mistake is made, it can't be undone. You see shattered glass and don't know how to fix it. Living with shame holding your hand causes you to cry over the broken window while thinking it can never be repaired. Living a mended life helps you pick up those broken pieces and make a beautiful stained glass window. In this instance, that stained glass is an apology, a teachable lesson, and then laughing together on the floor. Some of my personal stained glass pieces look like giving marriage advice on a podcast, writing this book, or helping a woman overcome alcohol addiction...all the while knowing the past me may not have been "qualified" to do any of that. The past me was too full of regret and too "bad" to do good things in the world. Having a mended life leaves no room for the devil to fill your heart with lies.

I surprise myself sometimes when I tell the Devil to go to hell and bust through the narrative I had always spoken to myself. I am committed to destroying shame, the Devil, and that past narrative, so I keep putting in the work. But in all honesty, I thought this walk would be a little easier. I hoped that it would be. This forgiveness, goal-setting, foundation-building, working through the hard times, and preparing for some type of heartache is exhausting in many ways. When I think about it from the perspective of the massive amount of energy it takes to live intentionally, I don't like it. When I look at it from the way my life looks now and the way my heart feels because of it, I would do it a million times over. I have smiled and loved and laughed and forgiven so much in the past few years that, somehow, it is becoming normal for me to wake up and love my life. Life can be good. It may never be easy, but it can be good.

As you've already read, I have had some really "good" times in my life. In the bigger picture, when comparing it to everyone in the world, I have always had a really good life. But my mentality of good has always heavily relied on what my external circumstances were.

Life was good when I was baptized. Life was good when I made the soccer team and got an acceptance letter to college. Life was good because I had four beautiful babies and a husband. Life is good taking vacations and enjoying the beach without alcohol.

Life was bad when my dad left. Life was bad when my mom took a bottle of pills. Life was bad when my boyfriend broke up with me. Life was bad when I made the choice to have an abortion that I deeply regretted. Life was bad when my grandma died, and I drowned my grief with alcohol. What if I told you that as good or bad as those circumstances are, they aren't the types of things that determine if your life is good? Nothing external gets to have a place in what is rooted in your heart. That's between you and God. Seriously. I'm not undermining your grief. I promise I am not. Things can be bad. Really bad. Yet, when you have eternal hope in your heart, you don't have to dwell on any worldly problem. It is imperative to know that God "will wipe away every tear from their eyes; there shall be no more death, nor sorrow, nor crying. There shall be no more pain, for the former things have passed away"

(Revelation 21:4, NKJV). Living by this scripture renews my strength as I continue through this life. Things are good. If I am judging my life by worldly standards, I would still say things are good. But just like the little voice once told me six years ago, this will come to pass. Hard times are guaranteed to come again. I can't see the future, so I can't say that I won't struggle again. I can tell you I will carry this verse with me as long as I am on Earth. I will live with a hope in my heart that even if things don't end in the way I hope, my end is with eternity. Every tear will be dry, and crying, mourning, sickness, and death will be no more.

My story will always end with hope.

Where will yours end? The process of mending your life is relentless, and if you are working to mend yours, you know this is true. Every day is a choice. On the good days, you have a choice to soak up those moments or focus on the negative parts of your day/life. On the bad days, you have a choice to sit in the pain or have hope for a better tomorrow, whenever your tomorrow may be. The resolution you're hoping for may not actually be tomorrow. It may be many tomorrows, but one day, you will see why things worked out the way they did. On the days when you have chosen the option you shouldn't have, you have a choice to let shame take your hand or to push it away. I won't hope that you always make the right decisions on your good or bad days because we all make mistakes sometimes. I will, however, hope that you push away the shame. Pick up the broken pieces, and mend them into something beautiful, piece by piece.

Why Does This Even Matter?

Do you really want to know why this matters? Why

am I telling you every part of my story and breaking down the lesson from it to give to you?

Because your life matters.

Your happiness matters, your family matters, and the generations after you matter. It has been such an honor to share every detail with you so *you* can wake up, put your feet on the ground, and keep going. The past few years have been some of the best for me. Yes, because things are going smoothly at the moment. Once I let go of that shame and changed my perspective to one of hope, I could see a future. That's the future I want you to see. I want you to wake up with a fire that burns so bright the Devil can't put it out. I want you to envision a beautiful life and have the guts to run to it. That's a big reason why there is joy in my heart. I can see a future. It isn't a celebrity's future or a fairy-tale future. It is mine. I know it might be a lifetime away, but I know if I keep going, it might one day be my own. Abundant joy is our future. I'm running after it at full speed, and I want you to do that too.

So how do we continue to run toward that dream when we have done all of this work? We have forgiven ourselves. We have hope for our futures…but life still feels mundane, bleak, and hard?

Life application for this chapter:

Step 1: Take up your cross daily.

The Bible recounts Jesus' exact words when He said, "If anyone would come after me, let him deny himself and take up his cross daily and follow me" (Luke 9:23, ASV).

This book is full of stories from my past ranging from twenty years ago to one year ago. Since finishing the book, I am sure I have made a few more mistakes that I could write about.

I feel like so many people have this idea that once a month has passed, or a year, or a decade in which you haven't given in to that bad decision, then you can say you have conquered it. But what if you don't make it that long? I've woken up committed to being a patient and loving mom, and then snapped at my daughter within a minute of her being awake. Does that mean we aren't ready for our good life and good future yet? Does it mean that maybe we need to read a few more self-help books before we really change? No. The Bible doesn't say to take up your cross once and be changed for life. It says to "deny himself and take up his cross *daily*" (Luke 9:23, ASV). Dying to yourself daily means that every single time you mess up, you humble yourself, knowing that only the strength of Jesus can carry you through your struggles. This verse exemplifies how even Jesus, perfect and complete, knew we would mess up. He knew we would mess up often. He knew that only His grace would be enough to pick us back up to try again…and again…and again.

If we are being told by our Creator to die DAILY to our sins, then we should do it! There is no reason to hold on to the failures of yesterday's mistakes. There are days when I have to take up my cross hourly. To give it to Jesus, ask for His strength, and immediately try again. To grow as a person is to realize what isn't serving you and do better the next time. With every next move that is just slightly better than the one before, your life can turn into something so much better than you could ever even imagine! Let Jesus be your guide.

Step 2: Monitor progress. Don't strive for perfection.

We are in the trenches of fighting for a better life. We have our goal in mind, and we know what sacrifices it will take to get there. When you wake up with that in mind, and you are fully focused on the end results, man; it is easy to keep the momentum going. What about when you slip and mess up? What happens on the bad days when you give in to the old, negative coping mechanisms?

I've tried so many diets in my life. I believe I started dieting to some degree by the time I was twelve years old. In those eighteen years since starting dieting to now, I have never made it past day four, even with the easiest diets, like not eating fast food. Every time, I would mess up on day four (or *hour four*, if we are being honest). I would completely stop the diet. I would believe that because I messed up once, it was over. It always felt like such a waste of time and a big disappointment. When I wanted to stop drinking, however, I took a different approach. The first night I gave in and drank too much, I woke up with the familiar feeling of regret and disappointment. It almost seemed like instinct to drink again to cover up the regret. Instead, I looked at my successes instead of my failures. I had gone two weeks without drinking, and that was better than the month before. I messed up once, but I realized it was still an improvement. That boost of confidence made it easier for me to stick to my goal.

Make it your goal to look at your successes, not your failures. Look at how much you have progressed instead of the times you've slipped. You are changing your life. It won't be easy, and it won't be perfect. Every time you fall back to that addiction, snap at your husband, impulse buy that purse, eat the candy bar, sleep in, etc., it doesn't mean you've failed. It means you are human. Progress takes constant work. Be proud that even though it might be a little change, you are better than you once were.

Step 3: Share your story.

I don't have a massive following on social media. It's mostly composed of people I know in the real world. Any post or picture I share, I typically get 50-ish likes and 5 to 10 comments. After Andy had successfully given up alcohol for several months, with his permission, I made a post congratulating him for his success. I included how much life had changed and told people that change is hard, but it is so worth it. That post got 350 likes and 80 comments. I was absolutely blown away. That's what the world is after. That is what people want to see! They need to see mess-ups, failures, hurts, and pain…not to judge you on it but to receive hope they can do it too! Honestly, it was an earth-shattering realization for me. *No one cares about what I did or what I went through. They want to know how I grew from it and how they can do it too.*

If you are still breathing, then you are on this earth for a purpose. You are still fighting for a reason. There are times when you might feel alone in this battle, but I promise you there is someone in the world who is trying to beat the same demons you have already overcome. The world needs *your story*. It doesn't matter how little or big it is. Every time you bring a secret to light, the devil can use it less and less because someone gets to use it for their own hope. Share your story. Change the world.

I hope you read this and see yourself in some part of my story. I know the details may differ, but many of the feelings have to be the same. My story is one of good and bad times, hope, worth, friends, love, mistakes, loss, overcoming, and forgiveness. I know you have some of the same characteristics in your story as well.

Over the years, I have bought so many books. I wanted

the quick fix. Every time I was in a bookstore, I would walk straight to the self-help section to see if maybe there was a book that could get me through this time. I have purchased books on every topic, from religion to trauma, addiction, parenting, and so much more. With almost every read, I would be captivated and inspired while reading it, but then as soon as it was over, I would swiftly fall back into my slump. Why? It wasn't because I wasn't willing to read and take notes. I did that with almost every book—highlighting and jotting down specific takeaways. I would fall back into my hopeless slump because I wasn't willing to read the notes, make changes, and take action. I didn't do the work. I wanted to do the work, but I didn't even know where to start.

When I wrote this book, I thought of myself and my struggles when reading a new self-help book. I thought about that hopeful excitement and then the swift letdown. I also thought about you. I couldn't possibly just tell you my story without telling you *how* I grew from those experiences. I also couldn't write a teaching book without telling you about all of the hardships I endured and mistakes I made along the way. You have read my story and read through the lifework. Do it. Go through the steps, do the work, and let it change your life. The word mended has several definitions. My favorite is "to restore to health or to heal." You deserve that. You deserve the healing. You deserve health—a peaceful mind, abundant joy, and healthy relationships. Take whatever brokenness you have and pick it up. It isn't the end for you. It is the beginning of something new and beautiful. Put your pieces back together, and create your new life. My friend, it is your time to be **mended.**

MENDING.

NOTES

1. Glennon Doyle, "The Gift That Comes from Hitting Rock Bottom," oprah.com from the June 2017 issue of O, The Oprah Magazine.

2. Centers for Disease Control and Prevention. "Suicide and Occupation." Center for Disease Control and Prevention. CDC, last modified August 8, 2019. Access date April 25, 2021. https://www.cdc.gov/niosh/topics/stress/suicide.html.

3. Alli Worthington, "Beth Moore on fruitfulness, calling, and staying strong," interview with Beth Moore, The Alli Worthington Show, podcast audio, August 10, 2020, https://alliworthington.com/bethmoore/.

4. James Clear, Atomic Habits: An Easy & Proven Way to Build Good Habits & Break Bad Ones.
Penguin Publishing Group, 2018.

5. "Forgive." Merriam-Webster.com. https://www.merriam-webster.com/dictionary/forgive. Accessed: October 22, 2020.

6. Smedes, Lewis B. Forgive and Forget: Healing the Hurts We Don't Deserve. San Francisco, CA: HarperSanFrancisco, 2007.

ABOUT THE AUTHOR

Riki-Leigh has been a writer her entire life. Writing has been her form of escape, healing, and dreaming since she was a little girl. What started as diary entries about boys, friends, and life-dreams transformed to blog entries about her growing family and the struggles of being a new mom and wife. Two decades later, her first book is about what she knows best- the hard stuff.

Littered through those diary and blog entries were her struggles and the overall question of, "How do I grow from this?" Her first book, Mended, is based directly from that. Writing about the hard stuff, the stuff that no one wants to talk about is her specialty. There's no topic off limits and no struggle that can't be turned into a lesson.

Mended is her first book baby, but not her last. Riki-Leigh has dreams to publish many more in the future. Her most important goal is to lead women through the hard stuff knowing that God is always in control and using their story for the good.

Riki-Leigh lives in coastal South Carolina with her 4 beautiful children and husband of 12 years. Her jobs include, but not limited to, pharmacist, writer, secretary, chauffeur, homework helper, and snack maker. She enjoys Bible studies, running, and true crime podcasts.

You can find her on instagram at @RL.Harnish or visit her website at www.mendthismess.com

CPSIA information can be obtained
at www.ICGtesting.com
Printed in the USA
LVHW020837090622
720769LV00014B/1490

9 781952 840180